Comptroller of the Currency
Administrator of National Banks

Merchant Processing

Comptroller's Handbook

December 2001

A

Assets

Merchant Processing

Introduction

Merchant processing[1] is the **settlement** of electronic payment transactions for merchants. Merchant processing activities involve gathering sales information from the merchant, obtaining **authorization** for the transaction, collecting funds from the card-issuing bank, and reimbursing the merchant. The processing of sales transactions for merchants by banks does not directly affect the bank's balance sheet except through settlement accounts and reserve balances. However, merchant processing can create significant off-balance-sheet contingent liabilities that may result in losses to the bank.

Most merchant processing transactions originate from retail credit card purchases, but **debit card purchases**, smart card purchases, and **electronic benefits transfer (EBT)** transactions are increasing sources of processing volume. In recent years, **bankcard associations** have aggressively promoted the move to electronic transactions through their **interchange rate** structure. Because of this and advances in technology, the vast majority of credit card sales transactions are now electronic.

Merchant processing is a business of high volumes and low profit margins. Generally, a high level of sales and transaction volume is needed to create a profitable operation as a result of the low income generated per transaction. Processing high transaction volume carries risk; only efficiently run departments can successfully maintain the necessary cost controls and effectively manage the accompanying transaction and credit risks.

As a high-volume business, merchant processing is dominated by a relatively few large and midsize banks, which often use the services of **independent sales organizations** or **membership service providers** (ISOs/MSPs), join partnerships/alliances, or enlist **agent banks**. These dominant banks are intensely competitive, and they price aggressively. To create economies of scale, they have steadily increased the volume of their merchant processing during the past 10 years.

---

[1] Bolded terms are defined in the glossary.

Some bankers do not understand merchant processing and its risks. Attracted to the business by the potential for increased fee income, they may underestimate the risks and not employ personnel with sufficient knowledge and expertise. They also may not devote sufficient resources to oversight or perform proper due diligence reviews of **third-party organizations**. As well, many banks simply do not have the managerial experience, resources, or infrastructure to safely engage in merchant processing outside their local market or to manage high sales volume, high-risk merchants, or high **chargeback** levels.

This handbook will focus on card payment-related processing, which is a separate and distinct line of business from credit card issuing.

Types of Merchant Processors

The role and accompanying risks of banks and third-party organizations varies. The most common participants in merchant processing are acquiring banks, agent banks with and without liability, and third-party organizations.

Acquiring Banks

A bank that contracts with merchants for the settlement of credit card transactions is an acquiring bank or an acquirer. Acquiring banks contract directly with the merchant, or indirectly through agent banks or other third-party organizations, to process credit card transactions.

Agent Banks with Liability

Agent banks contract with merchants on behalf of an acquiring bank. Agent banks are typically community banks that do not directly offer merchant processing services to their merchant customers. These banks refrain from contracting with merchants on their own because they lack the management expertise or the necessary infrastructure needed to serve as an acquirer.

Acquiring banks generally provide all **backroom operations** to the agent bank and own the **bank identification number** (BIN)/**Interbank Card Association**

(ICA) number through which settlement takes place. A BIN/ICA number is an individual member's unique identification number that facilitates clearing and settlement through Visa and MasterCard. Depending upon the contractual arrangement with the acquirer, the agent bank may be liable in the event of chargeback or fraud losses.

Agent Banks without Liability (Referral Banks)

Many community banks have referral arrangements with acquirers. In a referral arrangement, the acquirer performs the underwriting, executes the merchant agreement, and accepts responsibility for merchant losses. The acquiring bank may pay the referring bank a fee for brokering the merchant relationship.

Agent banks occasionally refer or want to sign merchants that do not meet the acquirer's underwriting guidelines. The acquirer may accept the account on the condition that the agent bank signs an agreement indemnifying the acquirer against losses. When a referral bank indemnifies the acquirer for losses, it becomes an agent bank with liability for those merchants indemnified. Indemnification agreements are typically used when the agent bank has other account relationships with the merchant and, as a customer service, wants to assist them in obtaining processing services. Bank management and examiners should be familiar with the limits on a national bank's ability to indemnify a transaction, as outlined in 12 CFR 7.1017.

Third-Party Organizations

Third-party organizations include any outside company the acquiring bank contracts with to provide merchant processing services. In addition to soliciting merchants, ISOs/MSPs may perform such services for acquirers as processing merchant applications, processing chargebacks, detecting fraud, servicing merchant customers, providing accounting services, selling/leasing electronic terminals to merchants, processing transactions, authorizing purchases, and capturing data.

Acquiring banks frequently outsource functions to third-party organizations to control costs. An acquirer's sales and transaction volume may not justify the cost of in-house data processing, or the bank may not want to staff a direct sales force. Acquirers can benefit from the technological expertise and capabilities of third parties without having to develop the systems and infrastructure themselves. Third-party organizations provide a wide array of services; examiners should understand that each acquirer's list of third parties used and services outsourced will be unique.

Acquiring banks sometimes receive third-party services indirectly. For example, an ISO/MSP may contract directly with a data processor or network provider, and the ISO/MSP passes the service onto the bank. Banks can also receive services indirectly through an ISO/MSP that contracts with another ISO/MSP to provide services.

There are hundreds of third parties providing services, and the quality of the services can vary widely. Banks should exercise strong due diligence and maintain strong vendor management programs for third-party organizations.

Association Requirements

Because third-party organizations are not bankcard association members, each acquirer must register its third-party organizations with the bankcard associations before it can accept their services. The acquirer must pay an initial registration fee and annual fees to the bankcard associations for each third party under contract. This fee is normally passed on to the third party.

After registration, the acquirer remains responsible for complying with the bankcard association's operating regulations on business relationships with third parties. These regulations make the acquiring bank liable to the bankcard associations for the actions of its third parties. The bankcard associations also require acquiring banks to regularly submit information on their third-party organizations. Acquiring banks can be fined for failing to provide the information.

Rent-a-BIN

The **rent-a-BIN** discussion below focuses on merchant processing (acquiring) rent-a-BIN arrangements. There are also credit card (issuing) rent-a-BIN relationships with similar requirements for strong vendor management and oversight programs; however, the issuing rent-a-BIN has its own set of unique risks and operations outside the scope of this handbook.

Rent-a-BIN describes an arrangement in which an acquiring bank permits ISO/MSPs to use the bank's BIN/ICA number to settle merchant credit card transactions. The bank has minimal operational involvement. The ISO/MSP retains the majority of income, and the bank receives a fee for the use of the BINs/ICAs.

The acquiring bank that owns the BIN/ICA number always retains risk of loss as well as responsibility for settlement with the associations. Banks are held responsible based on the contractual provisions of the association membership. Therefore, bank management should rigorously oversee and control these arrangements to ensure that the ISO/MSP is appropriately managing the risk. Oversight controls are important, even if the ISO/MSP shares in the liability. Moreover, the acquiring bank must consider any lending relationships the bank has with ISOs/MSPs in analyzing the bank's total risk exposure.

Refer to discussions on third-party organizations and ISOs/MSPs in the "Primary Risks" section (Strategic, Credit, and Transaction) and "Risk Management and Controls" (Third-Party Organizations) section of this booklet for additional information.

Operations

This section summarizes how a credit card transaction is processed. The intricacies may vary significantly for each institution, but the basic principles will be the same.

Authorizing Transactions

To authorize credit card transactions, the merchant obtains approval from the card-issuing bank or from a third party approved by the card-issuer. This authorization process is structured to prevent transactions being approved for cardholders who have not satisfactorily maintained their credit card account or who are over their credit limit, as well as to protect against the unauthorized use of stolen and fraudulent cards.

Typically, the clerk at the point of sale swipes the credit card through a terminal to obtain the information stored on the magnetic stripe on the back of the card, then inputs the amount of the transaction. This information is then transmitted to the merchant bank or its processor, who captures the transaction and forwards the information to the card-issuing bank through the bankcard association network. Depending on the status of the cardholder's account, the transaction will be approved or declined, and this decision will be transmitted back through the bankcard association network to the point of sale. After the transaction is authorized, the clerk prints a sales draft that the customer signs.

Acquiring banks now require authorizations for all **paper-based transactions**. Having each transaction authorized helps protect the merchants against fraudulent transactions. The authorizations have also eliminated the need for paper-based warning bulletins.

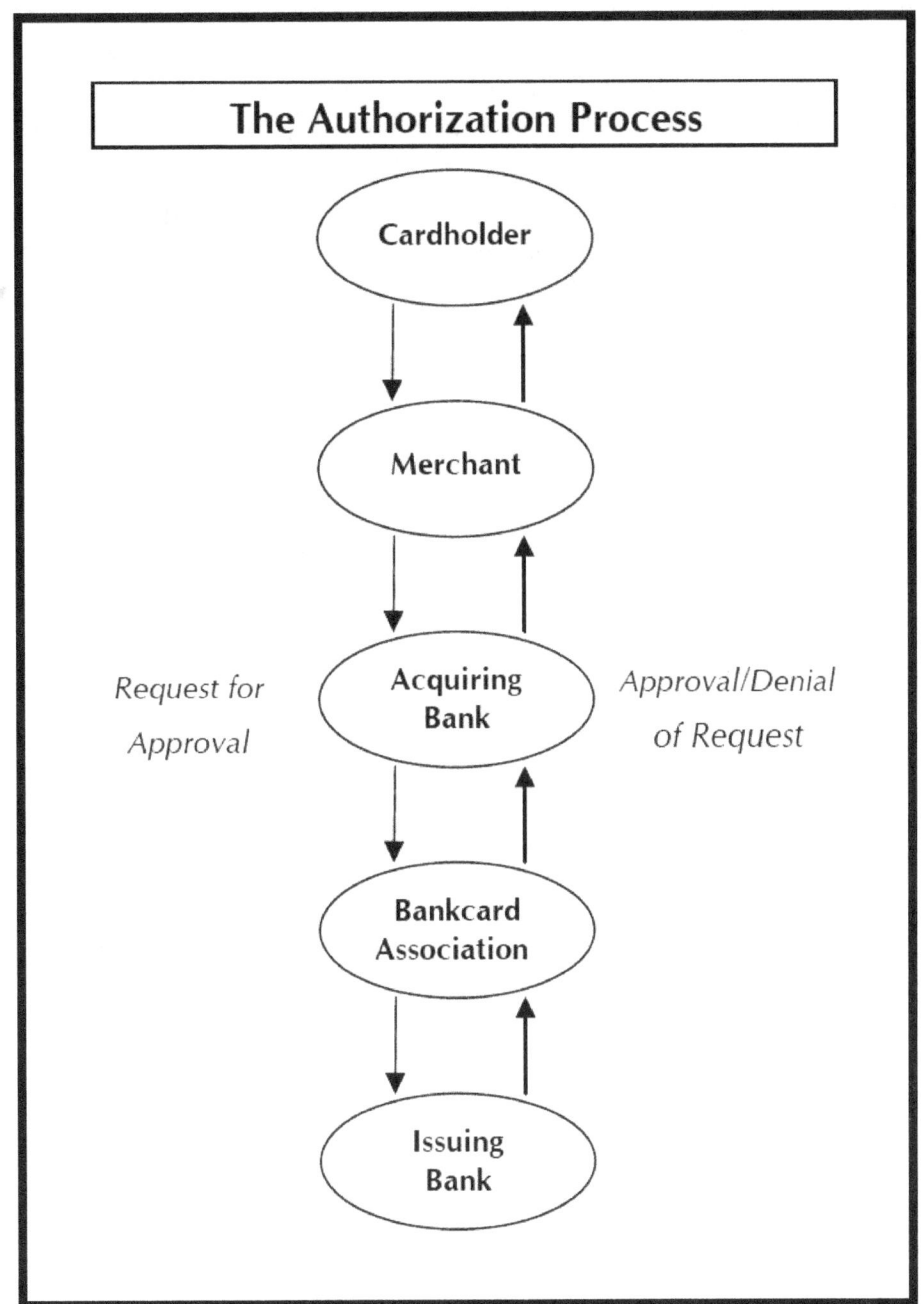

The Authorization Process

Cardholder

Merchant

Request for Approval   Acquiring Bank   Approval/Denial of Request

Bankcard Association

Issuing Bank

Settlement

Settlement is the process of transmitting sales information to the card-issuing bank for collection and reimbursement of funds to the merchant. A typical transaction flows from the merchant to the acquirer (or acquirer's processor), then to the bankcard associations, and finally to the card-issuing bank (or its processor), who bills the cardholder. Funds flow in the opposite direction from the card-issuing bank to the bankcard associations, then to the acquirer, and finally to the merchant. An acquiring bank's outsourcing of some (and sometimes all) of its merchant processing to third parties complicates transaction flows and fund flows.

A merchant submits sales transactions to its acquirer by either of two methods. The computers of large merchants often transmit directly to the acquirer or its third-party processor. Smaller merchants usually submit data to a third-party vendor that collects data from several merchants. The vendor then transmits transactions to the acquirers.

The acquiring bank transmits the information through **interchange** to the issuing banks. The issuers remit funds, through the bankcard associations, to the acquirer and post the charges to the cardholders' accounts. After the acquirer receives proceeds, it pays the individual merchants. Most third-party processors net settle with their clients. That is, a bank receives, or pays, the net of merchant and cardholder activity for each day of business.

Acquirers should limit the settlement risk by paying merchants after receiving credit from the card-issuing bank. For select merchants, the bank may pay the merchant prior to receipt of funds through interchange, thereby increasing the bank's credit and liquidity exposure. Timing of the payments to the merchants is specified in the agreement between the acquirer and the merchant. The agreement should always allow the bank to review the transaction for fraud prior to releasing funds. The acquirer should not become reliant on the merchant's deposits to fund other bank activities.

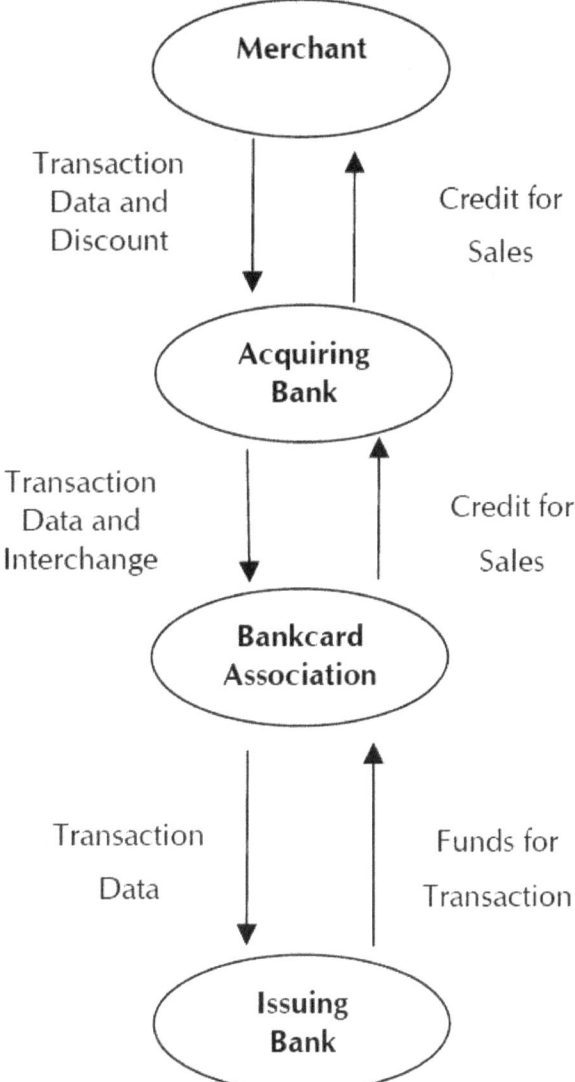

Clearing and Settlement Process[1]

Merchant

Transaction Data and Discount

Credit for Sales

Acquiring Bank

Transaction Data and Interchange

Credit for Sales

Bankcard Association

Transaction Data

Funds for Transaction

Issuing Bank

[1]This diagram provides a basic overview of the process. The timing of the discount and interchange fees may not directly correspond with the transfer of transaction data as depicted (i.e., discount is commonly collected on a monthly basis and interchange is generally collected on a daily basis at net settlement). Also, this diagram does not illustrate the complexities to the process added by using third-party organizations.

Fedwire

The card-issuing bank pays the bankcard associations using Fedwire, a real-time funds transfer system. In order to use the Fedwire, banks must hold accounts at the Federal Reserve Bank; settlement funds come from these accounts. The card-issuing bank makes the payment by sending a message over the Fedwire authorizing the Federal Reserve Bank to electronically debit its account at the Federal Reserve Bank for the net settlement amount and to transfer the funds to the bankcard association's settlement bank. These transfers are essentially instantaneous. The bankcard association's settlement bank then pays the acquiring bank using the Fedwire.

Automated Clearing House (ACH)

Acquirers usually pay merchants by initiating automated clearinghouse (ACH) credits to merchants' deposit accounts at the merchants' local banks. If an acquirer employs a third-party processor, the processor usually prepares the ACH file. Management should have controls in place to ensure that these ACH transactions are accurate. Bank employees should follow formal procedures when delaying settlement of a merchant's funds. Such a delay usually occurs because fraud staff finds a transaction suspicious or unusual. Placing a hold on funds affects the origination of the ACH file. See OCC Advisory Letter 2001-3, "Internet-Initiated ACH Debits/ACH Risks."

Chargeback Processing

Chargebacks are common in the merchant processing business, and a merchant must be capable of paying them. If the merchant is out-of-business or otherwise unable to pay the chargebacks, the acquiring bank suffers the loss.

Transaction Flow

Cardholders initiate chargebacks when they are dissatisfied with merchandise or a service, when they never received the merchandise or service, or when they never authorized the charge.[2] A consumer must first try resolving the dispute with the merchant. If unsuccessful, the consumer informs his or her card-issuing bank of the dispute, then the card-issuing bank posts a temporary credit to the cardholder. The card-issuing bank requests documentation from the merchant that authenticates the transaction and possibly resolves the dispute. If the chargeback is upheld, the amount is charged back to the merchant's account, and the consumer does not pay for the disputed charge. The customer has 60 days[3] from the day the statement is received to report a dispute to the card-issuing bank.

Card-issuing banks can also initiate chargebacks when the merchant does not follow proper card acceptance and authorization procedures (e.g., no authorization obtained or card used after expiration date). The acquirer incurs contingent liability for as many as 180 days.

Bankcard associations have strict chargeback processing regulations. For example, an association allows banks to charge transactions back to a merchant when the merchant fails to provide copies of requested sales tickets. If the merchant does not fulfill a requested item (**retrieval request**) within a prescribed time, it will lose the chargeback dispute. The merchant must have a process to respond to retrieval requests and chargeback investigations in a timely manner.

---

[2] The reasons for chargebacks listed are merely examples. There are many other reasons for chargebacks.

[3] Sixty days is the time allowed under federal consumer regulations (Regulation Z and Regulation E); however, the bankcard associations may allow more time to initiate a chargeback.

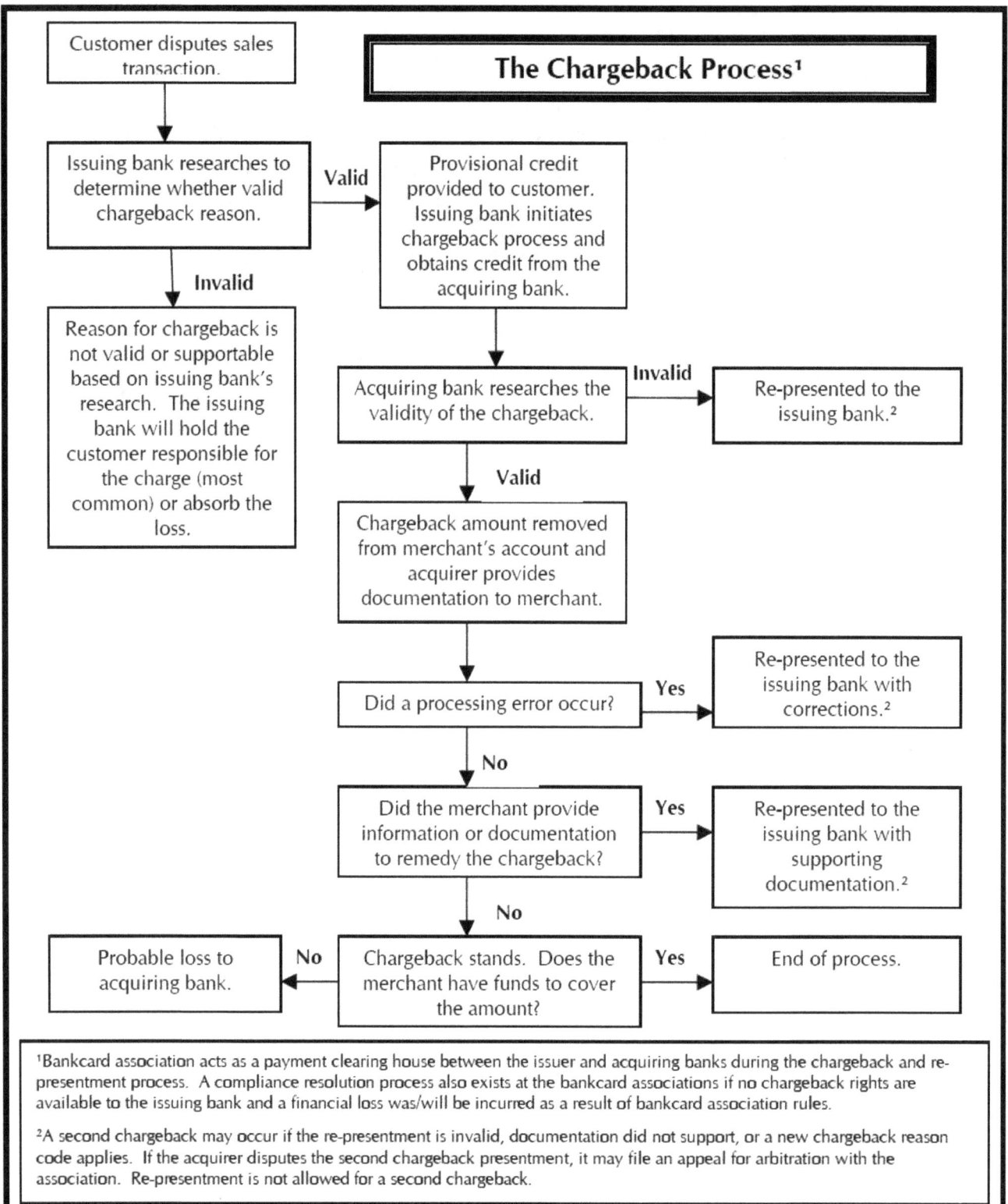

The Chargeback Process[1]

Customer disputes sales transaction.

↓

Issuing bank researches to determine whether valid chargeback reason. —**Valid**→ Provisional credit provided to customer. Issuing bank initiates chargeback process and obtains credit from the acquiring bank.

Invalid
↓

Reason for chargeback is not valid or supportable based on issuing bank's research. The issuing bank will hold the customer responsible for the charge (most common) or absorb the loss.

Acquiring bank researches the validity of the chargeback. —**Invalid**→ Re-presented to the issuing bank.[2]

Valid
↓

Chargeback amount removed from merchant's account and acquirer provides documentation to merchant.

↓

Did a processing error occur? —**Yes**→ Re-presented to the issuing bank with corrections.[2]

No
↓

Did the merchant provide information or documentation to remedy the chargeback? —**Yes**→ Re-presented to the issuing bank with supporting documentation.[2]

No
↓

Probable loss to acquiring bank. ←**No**— Chargeback stands. Does the merchant have funds to cover the amount? —**Yes**→ End of process.

[1]Bankcard association acts as a payment clearing house between the issuer and acquiring banks during the chargeback and re-presentment process. A compliance resolution process also exists at the bankcard associations if no chargeback rights are available to the issuing bank and a financial loss was/will be incurred as a result of bankcard association rules.

[2]A second chargeback may occur if the re-presentment is invalid, documentation did not support, or a new chargeback reason code applies. If the acquirer disputes the second chargeback presentment, it may file an appeal for arbitration with the association. Re-presentment is not allowed for a second chargeback.

Fraud Detection

Every acquirer should have an antifraud system to monitor each merchant's daily activity. An acquiring bank is potentially liable for the fraud losses perpetrated by the merchant, including merchant's engaged in deceptive or misleading practices. A merchant can also directly defraud banks by such means as **factoring** and draft **laundering**. Management's ability to quickly detect merchant fraud is important in controlling the acquiring bank's losses. A merchant's fraud can be extremely costly if not discovered quickly.

Merchant fraud detection systems may also help identify cardholder fraud through the transaction monitoring. However, the credit card issuer is primarily responsible for detecting cardholder fraud.

Pricing

A key to successful and profitable merchant processing is properly setting the fees (pricing) the merchant will be charged for sales transactions and acquirer services. Merchant pricing is extremely competitive, especially on large and national-scale merchants who generate high transaction volume.

The acquiring bank may use various methods to price the merchant. Smaller merchants are frequently priced with a single **discount rate** based on merchant volume and average sales ticket. Acquiring banks frequently use unbundled pricing for their medium-sized and large merchants. When pricing is unbundled, fees are charged separately for each service. Fees on interchange, authorizations, and chargebacks may be unbundled. Other bank fees that may be unbundled include statement preparation, application fee, customer service, membership, maintenance, and penalty fees (for violation of association rules).

The pricing method chosen for a specific merchant should take into account the level of risk posed by the merchant. Pricing for higher-risk merchants (e.g., card not present, delayed delivery) may be set higher than for lower-risk merchants.

Many acquirers use a pricing model to determine their target discount rate. Acquirers may maintain several different pricing models. The model used depends on criteria in the bank's pricing policy such as the merchant's sales volume or merchant's type of business. Pricing models allow the acquirer to quickly input different variables for different sales volumes, average sales tickets, revenues, or expenses; the adjustments are designed to produce a desired profit margin. The pricing model should include all direct and indirect expenses. The accuracy of any pricing model depends upon reasonable assumptions for revenue and expenses.

Pricing Components

Discount Rate

Acquiring banks assign a discount rate for each merchant account at the time the merchant agreement is signed. In the most simplistic case, the **discount** represents a single rate charged a merchant based on the individual merchant's sales volume. For example, a merchant with a 2 percent discount rate will receive $98 for a $100 credit card sale processed with its acquiring bank. The discount is generally charged monthly to the merchant. This creates a timing difference because the bank is settling interchange with the associations on a daily basis. In other words, the bank in most cases pays the interchange charges prior to receiving payment for these charges from the merchant. This timing difference creates a credit exposure for the bank on the discount payable from the merchant.

Most merchant agreements allow the acquiring bank to change the discount rate for various cost increases. The most typical change is passing along new interchange rates set by the associations. The discount rate generally ranges from 1 percent to 4 percent for smaller to medium-sized merchants. Discount rates for high-volume merchants may be less than 1 percent, and many large merchants will be priced using unbundled pricing rather than a discount rate. Merchants who use **electronic data capture** are charged lower discount rates than paper-based merchants.

Management should be able to explain major deviations from their minimum discount rates. Banks often give a favorable discount rate to merchants that are commercial borrowers or deposit holders. A merchant's discount rate can also be favorable because the merchant leases credit card equipment from the bank. Although setting prices based on other services or relationships is an acceptable practice, the bank should be able to measure the overall profitability of a merchant account. The examiner should review discount rates for insiders to ensure that they don't receive better rates and terms than similar bank customers.

Interchange Fees

An **interchange fee** is compensation paid by the acquiring bank to the issuing bank via bankcard associations for the transaction passing through interchange. Therefore, interchange is an expense on the acquirer's income statement and income on the issuer's income statement.

Associations set interchange rates on a periodic basis (generally once per year in April). There are numerous interchange rates relating to factors such as the type of authorization (e.g., card present or card not present) and type of business (e.g., grocery store). The bank's pricing must consider the different interchange rates when pricing merchants.

Processing Fees

The processing fee varies with the size and number of transactions the merchant submits per batch, and covers the costs associated with data processing services required for the transaction. The processing fee may include data capture and authorization costs. The fee may go directly to the bank if it does all the processing or to the bank's third-party processor.

ISO/MSP Fees

The ISO/MSP fee is the amount the acquiring bank pays the ISO/MSP for services provided. These services usually include soliciting merchants and customer service. The ISO/MSP fee is negotiated and often represents a percentage of the volume the ISO/MSP-sponsored merchants bring to the bank. The examiner should determine that pricing for merchants signed by

ISOs/MSPs is consistent with the fee agreement between the bank and the ISO/MSP.

Agent Bank Commission

The agent commission is a fee passed on to the agent bank for signing a merchant. This fee is either built into the discount rate or charged separately.

Other Income

Discount income is not the only way banks generate fee income. Other programs include equipment leasing, merchant clubs offering unlimited supplies, travel agency services, and term life insurance. Management should make sure that any products and services offered comply with applicable laws and regulations.

Primary Risks

Merchant processing can be a safe and profitable business if bank management properly understands and controls the strategic, credit, and transaction risks, which are significant. A failure to control these risks brings compliance, reputation, and liquidity risks into the mix.

Strategic Risk

Bank management must decide whether merchant processing activities are consistent with the bank's overall business plan and strategic direction. If a bank's capital base is limited in relation to existing or projected sales volume, the bank may lack the financial capacity to support the level of risk.

The board and management of any bank considering whether to undertake merchant processing or to maintain or expand its merchant processing business must be fully aware of the risks involved. Management should identify the business's risks as well as the expertise and controls that will be required to manage them. They should determine how well the bank can keep pace with technology and competition. And they should determine such matters as what industries to pursue and how much to use third-party organizations.

Strategic considerations should include:

- The current business environment to determine whether the line of business can be managed safely and profitably.

  As previously stated, merchant processing is dominated by a small group of institutions that have the experience, resources, and infrastructure to process nearly any type and size of merchant, from the small main street businesses to the largest nationwide retailers. These acquirers' economies of scale allow them to compete on service and price. Intense pricing competition and improved technology have also resulted in low customer loyalty, and merchants can change processors virtually overnight.

- The need for a highly specialized and reliable infrastructure.

  The OCC expects banks to have risk management systems commensurate with an activity's risks. Management experience, staffing, systems, and reporting must be sufficient to enable the bank to monitor merchants' activities knowledgeably and effectively.

- The potential impact of the activity on earnings and capital.

  Management must consider the implications for capital of off-balance-sheet risk (e.g., fraud and chargeback exposure resulting from sales volume and higher risk merchants). Fraud and credit losses can occur quickly. The bank must determine whether its financial resources are adequate for the risk of merchant processing. **Depending upon the risk profile of the bank's merchant processing activities, the OCC may require capital above the regulatory minimums to support the risks of merchant processing.** Refer to the "Risk Management and Controls" (Capital) section of this booklet for additional information.

- The liability for fraud and chargeback losses and for bankcard association fines.

The ultimate contractual liability for losses lies with the bank that owns the BIN/ICA number. If the merchant or third party does not have the financial capacity to absorb the loss, the bank must absorb it. The bank that owns the BIN/ICA number is also contractually responsible for compliance with bankcard association requirements including services provided by a third party. Failure to comply with the bankcard association requirements can result in fines, security pledge requirements, and loss of bankcard association membership.

- The need for a strong vendor management program.

  Several banks have been financially impaired because of fraudulent and problem merchants signed by ISOs/MSPs. Uncontrolled growth, fraud, and inadequate operations by the third parties have all resulted in significant problems for banks. Before the bank accepts services from an ISO/MSP, it must implement policies, procedures, and controls to monitor the ISO/MSP's activities and to ensure that the ISO/MSP is operating within the guidelines established by the bank and bankcard associations.

  See the "Managing Third-Party Organizations" section of OCC Advisory Letter 2000-9, "Third-Party Risk," and OCC Advisory Letter 2000-12, "Risk Management of Outsourcing Technology Services," for additional information.

- The risk and reward analysis of whether the bank can generate adequate sales without taking unacceptable risks.

  The existence of high profits at lower volumes can indicate that the bank is processing for high-risk merchants. High profits may also indicate the bank is using third parties to conduct all activities without expending the resources to properly manage the business.

- The generation of deposits from the settlement of merchant processing activities.

Such deposits are highly volatile and are not a reliable source of funding, especially for a nationwide program. A common misconception is that such deposits will enable a bank to generate a profitable merchant processing business. In a nationwide program many, if not most, of the merchant account relationships will be at the merchant's primary bank, not the acquiring bank.

The bank must also consider the possible reputation risks involved in merchant processing. The bank's business decisions for marketing and pricing its service could affect its reputation in the marketplace. Reputation risk also exists in contractual obligations to merchants and third parties, as well as in the outsourcing of any part of merchant processing. Decisions made by the bank or by third parties acting on the bank's behalf can directly cause loss of merchant relationships, litigation, fines and penalties, and losses associated with chargeback reimbursements. An acquirer must perform strong due diligence of new third-party organizations and ongoing evaluation of third-party service standards and financial stability.

Credit Risk

Credit risk arising from chargebacks is a significant risk to an acquirer's earnings and capital. Although processing credit card transactions is technically not an extension of credit, the acquiring bank is relying on the creditworthiness of the merchant.

Merchant chargebacks become a credit exposure to the acquirer when either the merchant declares bankruptcy or is otherwise financially unable to pay. If a merchant cannot honor its chargebacks, the acquiring bank must pay the card-issuing bank. Banks have often been forced to cover large chargebacks when merchants have gone bankrupt or committed fraud. In many of these cases, the merchant engaged in deceptive or misleading practices. The contingent liability can span several months of the merchant's sales volume because of the cardholder's rights to dispute the charge and the chargeback process. Moreover, high-volumes of chargebacks may result in large fines from the associations.

A single merchant or ISO/MSP-related merchants can generate sufficient sales and subsequent chargebacks to result in substantial losses to the bank. Chargebacks from a fraudulent or problem merchant (or group of these merchants) can total hundreds of thousands of dollars per day. These chargebacks can translate into recognized losses to the acquiring bank if the merchant(s) or ISO/MSP is incapable of payment. Chargeback losses can deplete earnings and capital in a matter of days, causing a bank to fail.

Substantial credit risk can arise from the use of the bank's BIN/ICA number by ISOs/MSPs. The indemnification of losses by ISOs/MSPs is only as strong as the creditworthiness of the ISO/MSP and the creditworthiness of the merchants signed by the ISO/MSP. Many of the most serious merchant processing losses at banks have resulted from merchants solicited by ISOs/MSPs (even when ISOs/MSPs were contractually responsible for losses).

If an acquiring bank permits other bankcard association members to use its BIN/ICA number, it also assumes credit risk. The BIN/ICA number owner has primary responsibility to the bankcard association for any user's failure to perform. Using another member's BIN/ICA number is also risky. If the BIN/ICA number-owning bank fails to perform, the bankcard association may hold the users liable. Although sharing BINs/ICA numbers is less common than in the past, users could be liable for all activity in the BIN/ICA number if they are a member of the bankcard associations.

Transaction Risk

Acquiring banks are faced with transaction risk daily as they process credit card transactions for their merchants. This risk arises primarily from the settlement process. Settlement is the process of transmitting sales information to the card-issuing bank for collection and reimbursement of funds to the merchant. Transaction risk can also arise from a bank's failure to process a transaction properly, inadequate controls, employee error or malfeasance, a breakdown in the bank's computer system, or a natural catastrophe.

A failure anywhere in the transaction process can result in risks to the bank's earnings and capital. For example:

- Failure to monitor the merchant acceptance process (including those generated by ISO/MSP relationships) can result in significant operational and credit problems. These include possible bankcard association fines; credit, fraud, and operational losses; inadequate staffing and infrastructure; and reputation repercussions.

- Failure to process chargebacks properly and in a timely manner, as specified in the bankcard associations' rules, can result in operational and credit losses.

- Failure to provide adequate staffing for chargeback processing and fraud monitoring can result in preventable operational and credit losses that occurred because of high workloads. Workloads can change quickly depending on sales growth and chargeback volume.

- Failure to comply with bankcard associations' operating rules can bring substantial fines.

- Failure to monitor daily sales transactions can result in substantial operational losses from fraudulent activity.

- Failure or inability to provide timely transmission of funds to merchants or third parties can result in operational losses, reputation risk, and liquidity risk.

- Failure to monitor the service quality and fulfillment (e.g., sales, chargeback processing, fraud monitoring, customer service, or ACH file creation) provided by third-party organizations can result in operational and credit losses, fines, and a negative reputation.

- Failure to monitor and compare initial merchant activity and pricing with actual merchant activity and pricing can result in unprofitable operations.

Risk Management and Controls

This section focuses on the primary methods by which acquiring banks, agent banks, and referral banks control risk. The risk management processes and controls may vary from institution to institution.

Board and Management Supervision

The board and management must ensure that the bank has a comprehensive risk management process. This process should include written policies and procedures appropriate to the size and complexity of operations. Risk management must include a system for approving merchants and an ongoing program to monitor their credit quality and guard against their fraud. A sound internal control environment and audit culture must be established.

Management and staff should have knowledge and skills appropriate for the type and level of the risk being taken. For example, personnel responsible for processing chargebacks should possess a full understanding of bankcard association rules, and personnel responsible for approving merchant applications should be able to properly evaluate merchant credit worthiness and identify high-risk merchants. Staffing levels should be commensurate with the workload.

Risk measurement systems must be in place to operate, monitor, and control the activity effectively. Senior management and the board should regularly receive reports that enable them to gauge the department's risk. Key management reports detail new account acquisitions, account attrition, portfolio composition, sales volumes, chargeback volumes, chargeback aging, fraud, and department profitability.

Agent Banks

Agent banks should fully understand their financial liability for merchants' chargeback and fraud losses, as well as their responsibilities under the agreement with the acquirer. Agent banks with liability should establish

---

appropriate risk controls, including ongoing monitoring. Monitoring should include sales activity, chargebacks, and fraud investigations.

Referral Banks

Referral banks need only minimal controls in place to monitor their relationship with the acquirer. If management has made any indemnification agreements, more comprehensive controls and reporting should be established because the referral bank is accepting liability.

Capital

The bank should hold appropriate capital for merchant processing activities. The board and management should limit the bank's volume of merchant processing relative to its capital, its risk profile, and management's ability to monitor and control the risks of merchant processing. The capital allocation for merchant processing should be supported and documented.

Existing regulations do not assess a specific charge for merchant processing activities. However, capital regulations (12 CFR 3.10(d)) permit examiners to require additional capital to support the level of risk. Factors to consider include:

- Sales volume — present and planned.
- Type and location of merchants.
- Role and supervision of third parties.
- Expertise of management.
- Ability to identify, monitor, measure, and control risks.
- Skill of personnel.
- Level of chargebacks.
- Profitability of merchant processing.
- Risk profile of the bank.
- Adequacy of capital to support other lines of business.

Bankcard associations have definitive rules that limit the processing volume a member can generate relative to its capital, its concentrations of high-risk merchants, and its chargeback rates.

Security Pledges

The bankcard associations may require security pledges if in their opinion the pledges are necessary to protect the bankcard payment system. These security pledges can be large if the risk posed by the bank's merchant processing activities is high. Management should fully understand that the bankcard associations may have contractual rights to offset funds from the bank's settlement account without the bank's prior permission.

Merchant Underwriting and Review

Management should implement a formal merchant underwriting and approval policy to control credit risk. The policy should designate the types of merchants with which the bank is willing to conduct business as well as the criteria for selecting merchants (e.g., time in business, location, and sales volumes). The bank's policy should define what information each application should contain, such as type of business, location, and social security number/tax identification number. The policy should also stipulate what information is required in the merchant agreement. The merchant agreement should disclose all fees, define what the merchant will be required to do at point of sale, and require notification of ownership changes or substantive marketing and product changes. The policy also should outline the procedures and schedules for the periodic reviews of the financial status of the existing merchant base.

Underwriting Standards

The underwriting policy should require a background check of the merchant to support the validity of the business, creditworthiness of the merchant, and sales history. The bank's underwriting standards should require, at a minimum:

- An application signed by the merchant.
- A processing agreement signed by the merchant.
- A signed corporate resolution, if applicable.
- An onsite inspection report or verification of business.
- Credit bureau reports, as allowed by the Fair Credit Reporting Act, on the principal of the business.
- Financial statement or credit reports on the business.
- Analysis of the merchant's activity using recent monthly statements from the merchant's current or most recent processor, if possible.
- Verification of trade and bank references.
- Evidence the merchant is not on the **Member Alert to Control High Risk Merchants (MATCH)** list. Such a check is standard industry practice.

Review and Approval of Merchants

In the initial review of merchant applications, banks reject merchants that have a history of substantial chargeback volumes, are weak financially, or do not operate a valid business. The depth of the initial review should match the level of risk posed by the merchant. Many acquirers are moving toward a risk-based approach to merchant underwriting. "Lower risk" or "lower volume" merchants may require only a limited underwriting process while "higher risk" merchants undergo far greater analysis. Acquirers using risk-based underwriting typically use enhanced credit and fraud monitoring systems.

The bank should also establish criteria for reviewing applications from a merchant's other locations. These procedures may be abbreviated from the standard underwriting guidelines, but verification is necessary. Verification should ensure that the type of business is similar to the existing location and that the merchant owns the additional locations.

The bank should establish who can approve new accounts. To approve a merchant whose sales volume is high, a senior officer's authorization should be required. Commercial lending experts should assess the creditworthiness of large merchants.

The policy should address documentation requirements. If the acquiring bank uses information collected by ISOs/MSPs, the bank's policy should outline the quality of information required and the review procedures required.

Prohibited or Restricted Merchants

When evaluating the credit quality of a merchant, a bank must consider the line of business and any product being offered by the merchant. Bankcard associations segment businesses by activity, and acquiring banks should continually analyze their merchant base along similar lines. Most acquiring banks compile a list of prohibited or restricted merchants which describes the types of merchants they are unwilling to sign or are willing to sign only under certain circumstances.

Certain types of businesses are inherently more risky. For example, although there are many reputable mail order and telemarketing (commonly referred to as MO/TO or MOTO in the industry) merchants, these merchants have, in aggregate, displayed a much higher incidence of chargebacks. Also, the risk of chargeback is greater if the merchant sells goods or services for **future/delayed delivery**, such as airline tickets, health club memberships, or travel clubs. In such circumstances, customer disputes are not triggered until the date of delivery.

Many banks use **holdback** or reserve accounts to mitigate credit risk on higher risk merchants.

Internet Merchants

The Internet gives fraudulent businesses and businesses with minimal financial resources ready access to the public. Acquirers should conduct thorough underwriting reviews of Internet merchants using bank and trade verifications. During the underwriting process, credit analysts should determine whether heightened fraud and chargeback risk warrants the use of additional risk mitigation techniques, such as delaying settlement or establishing reserves.

Electronic commerce over the Internet poses privacy and security concerns that should be addressed in the initial underwriting. The bank should ensure the security of transactions as well as stored data. Secured servers and data encryption technologies (e.g., **Secured Socket Layers (SSL)**) help to protect data and transaction integrity.

For Internet merchants, underwriting standards should stipulate that the following information must appear on the Web site:

- Customer service number (toll-free preferable).
- E-mail address to contact the company.
- Statement on security controls.
- Delivery methods and timing.
- Refund and return policies.
- Privacy statements (permissible uses of customer information).

Periodic Review

The financial condition of "high-volume" and "high-risk" merchants should be continually monitored. The bank's policy should stipulate the frequency of reviews and the size of merchants requiring reviews. In determining the threshold for periodic reviews, the bank should consider volume, concentrations, high-risk industries, and chargeback history. Depending on the composition of the bank's portfolio, it may not be necessary to review smaller merchants periodically; the bank may be able to rely on sound underwriting guidelines at acquisition. Whether or not a merchant's credit is reviewed periodically, its transactions — and those of every merchant — should be monitored rigorously for such events as fraud and chargebacks. To screen portfolios periodically for troubled accounts, many acquirers now use information databases (e.g., databases of risk scores, bankruptcy filings, and fraud data).

When the merchant processing department and the commercial lending department both have relationships with a merchant, each should inform the other department about any change in that merchant's credit quality. For example, a merchant's unacceptable chargeback rate could indicate emerging problems of credit quality, and a merchant's problem loan probably signals that the risk the merchant poses to the merchant processing department has increased. The bank should include the merchant manager on the routing of the problem loan report. If credit information shows that the merchant's financial condition is deteriorating, the bank may want to reduce its risk exposure. For instance, when dealing with a financially unstable merchant, the bank may require a holdback reserve or security deposit.

Acquiring Bank Reviews of Agent Banks

Acquiring banks should periodically review the financial condition of agent banks assuming loss liability. The financial capacity of the agent bank should be consistent with the risk profile of its merchant portfolio and volume of merchant activity. The acquirer does not need to review periodically a referral bank's condition.

Agent Bank Merchant Underwriting

Agent banks with liability should have appropriate underwriting procedures in place. An acquiring bank will expect the agent bank to reimburse it for any losses sustained. The agent bank's management should refer to the acquiring bank's underwriting criteria when developing guidelines. Acquirers may decline merchants that agent banks refer if they pose undue risk or do not meet the acquirer's minimum standards.

The complexity of an agent bank's underwriting guidelines will depend on the type of merchants it targets. If the account base is limited to existing customers and sales volumes are low, written underwriting guidelines may be minimal. When accounts are higher risk or volume is high relative to the bank's capital base, more extensive guidelines are appropriate. Agent banks often have more stringent criteria for nonbank customers than bank customers.

Profit Analysis and Monitoring Pricing

To ensure that the pricing process is adequately controlled, a bank's pricing policies should address the methods used for pricing, authority levels, and repricing procedures. The pricing policy facilitates consistency in pricing practices and helps optimize profit margins.

Management should ensure that merchants are priced appropriately throughout the life of the contract. Banks should verify a merchant's projected volume and ticket size shortly after processing begins and periodically thereafter. It should ensure that the discount rate is in line with the application estimate and original pricing model assumptions. All significant merchants should be reviewed for repricing at least annually. If any merchants are unprofitable, they should be repriced. Most agreements allow acquirers to increase discount rates and fees at any time during the life of the contract.

Banks must have management information systems (MIS) in place to measure the profitability of the merchant processing department. The quality of MIS varies among banks. Information systems should detail key performance measures such as net income to sales and net income per item. Ideally, the bank's MIS should be able to segment profitability by merchant, acquisition channel, and industry.

An acquiring bank's merchant operation should produce a discrete income statement. The income statement should include all direct and indirect costs. Direct costs include internal data processing, merchant accounting, fraud and chargeback losses, personnel, and occupancy costs. Indirect costs may include corporate overhead expenses such as human resources, legal, and audit service. Refer to appendix C for a sample profit and loss statement.

Management and the board should be kept informed of the merchant department's profitability. The level of detail and frequency of reporting to the board is contingent on the size and risk profile of the operation in relation to the overall operations of the bank and its capital base.

Agent Bank Pricing and Profitability

An agent bank's pricing should be sufficient to recoup the fees charged by the acquirer as well as the agent bank's other costs. Depending on the size of the agent's merchant portfolio, separate profitability reports on this line of business may not be necessary. However, management should always be able to determine whether the service is profitable to the bank. If profits are insufficient, management should consider whether any other benefits of offering merchant processing services make up the difference.

Fraud Monitoring

Detection Methods

Banks must monitor for merchants' fraud. Fraud analysts should not rely exclusively on excess chargeback activity to identify fraud. The primary tool for detecting fraud is an exception report that details variances from parameters established at account set-up. Basic parameters may include daily sales volume, average ticket size, multiple purchases of the same dollar amount, multiple use of the same cardholder number, the percentage of transactions keyed versus the percentage swiped, and chargeback activity. A daily exception report will list the merchants that breach these parameters.

Most large-volume processors have exception parameters by industry or merchant type. To maximize the efficiency of staff and monitoring reports, management should periodically update parameters. The daily sales threshold may be set at a percent (e.g., 110 percent) of a prior time frame's activity (e.g., three months' average). Such a margin allows for normal growth of the merchant and compensates for seasonal sales patterns. Internet merchants may require a higher level of monitoring because of heightened fraud and chargeback risks associated with this sales channel. Banks should develop Internet merchant monitoring commensurate with risks associated with these merchants.

Many acquirers are taking advantage of developments in neural network technology. Firms marketing such products have designed complex computer programs that compare each transaction against the merchant's prior sales patterns. Such sophisticated products may be beyond the budgets of smaller merchant processors. Some acquirers may selectively route higher risk transactions through the neural network, subjecting the remaining sales volume to an exception report.

Many banks use scoring, bankruptcy, trade, and fraud databases to identify merchants that are more likely to falsify transactions because of weak finances or legal difficulties.

Bankcard associations prepare fraudulent activity reports for each acquiring bank. These reports should be used in coordination with the bank's fraud system as verification. Bankcard associations may require banks to document plans to correct unacceptable merchant sales practices. Additionally, associations provide educational material to acquirers and merchants regarding the latest techniques in fraud detection.

Investigations

Management should take swift action when it encounters suspicious sales. Its investigation may include verifying purchases with the card-issuing bank, or obtaining copies of paper-based transaction tickets from the merchant. An acquirer's quick response will help to minimize its and the card-issuer's losses, as well as to notify law enforcement agencies. On any day, staffing should be sufficient to determine whether any of that day's exceptions has the characteristics of a fraudulent transaction.

Merchant agreements should allow the acquirer to delay settlement of funds until questionable transactions are resolved. Once fraud is suspected, management must file a Suspicious Activity Report (SAR) with the Financial Crimes Enforcement Network (FinCEN). Additionally, the account of a fraudulent merchant should be terminated, and the merchant's name should be placed on the Member Alert to Control High Risk Merchants (MATCH). Other banks use this MATCH to determine whether to accept merchants.

Chargeback Monitoring

An acquirer must have strong controls in place to accurately process chargebacks and retrieval requests in a timely manner. The acquirer may lose a chargeback dispute (and lose the money involved) if it does not adhere to strict bankcard association regulations. The bankcard associations notify acquirers of merchants having excessive chargebacks. The associations may fine banks that have high levels of chargebacks or that do not handle chargebacks properly. Management can limit the chargeback compliance risk by establishing a structured chargeback processing system to monitor and handle merchant chargebacks.

An acquirer's risk management practices should detect merchants having high levels of chargebacks. Numerous chargebacks may indicate an unscrupulous merchant, or the merchant's need for additional training. Chargeback employees should be alert for merchants with excessive retrieval requests or chargebacks.

Larger merchant processors employ collectors to recover chargeback losses and other fees. A collector will seek remedy from the principals of the business through negotiations or civil action.

Risk Mitigation

To protect themselves from merchants that pose high risk or that have a history of chargebacks, many acquirers establish merchant reserve accounts or holdback reserves. Holdback reserves are also used to limit a bank's credit risk when the merchant's product or service involves future/delayed delivery. A bank can fund the reserve by setting aside a lump sum or by withholding a portion of each day's proceeds until a sum has been reached.

The bank may also fund a general reserve account, similar to the allowance for loan and lease losses (ALLL), for a portfolio of merchant accounts. Although similar to the ALLL, the general reserve for merchant losses should be classified as an "other liability" account and not commingled with the ALLL. The amount of the reserve is often based on the entire portfolio's contingent chargeback exposure. Accounting for the reserve should be in accordance with generally accepted accounting principles (GAAP).

Banks can also purchase insurance against chargebacks. This insurance is written as comprehensive protection against uncollectible chargebacks. Although the insurance is comprehensive, banks must follow strict guidelines in order to collect on the insurance in the event of loss. The insurance can cover nondelivery of the product; unauthorized mail order or telephone order transactions; use of counterfeit, lost, or stolen card numbers; the factoring of credit card transactions; misuse of cardholder's funds; misrepresentation on the merchant application; collusion between the independent sales representative and merchant; and merchants' deceptive and misleading methods of soliciting funds from cardholders.

Accounting

Examiners should ensure that chargeback losses are appropriately detailed on call reports as other noninterest expense. Any collected funds are to be reported as other noninterest income. Any uncollectable fees should be reversed from income in a timely manner.

Settlement Controls

Acquiring banks must understand and assess the risk to their payment systems from merchant processing activities. An assessment of payment systems should help management to understand the risks to the bank; to establish policies, procedures, and controls appropriate to these risks; and to develop an audit process to review compliance with policy.

Acquiring banks should have strong vendor management programs that include written agreements with all third parties involved in the settlement process. The agreements should detail responsibilities, payment arrangements and schedules, and contingency plans. Additionally, management should have proper monitoring controls in place over parties in the settlement process. Controls should include quality assurance, audits, onsite visits, performance reporting, and financial monitoring.

Bank management should periodically review settlement transmission reports for large merchants. These reports summarize the interchange rates charged by the bankcard associations for each transaction. The reports may assist in identifying merchants with abnormal interchange rates. Abnormal interchange rates may indicate problems with the merchant's terminals or software. Identifying and correcting the problems may result in savings for the merchant and acquiring bank.

The success of a payment system depends on the participants' credit quality and the system's operational reliability. Management may obtain third-party reviews from its processors. Also, management may request a copy of regulatory examination reports of its processor from the bank's primary regulatory agency.[4] Examiners and bank management should refer to OCC Banking Circular 235, "International Payment Systems Risk," OCC Advisory Letter 2000-9, "Third-Party Risk," and OCC Advisory Letter 2000-12, "Risk Management of Outsourcing Technology Services" for guidance in monitoring payment system risks.

Managing Third-party Organizations

Due Diligence

Banks should check the background of each principal of an ISO/MSP. The financial capacity of the ISO/MSP and its principals should also be analyzed to verify the organization's viability and capacity to absorb losses. Many acquirers obtain cash deposits from the ISO/MSP to support the contractual arrangement. Banks should review an ISO's financial condition periodically.

Contracts

Bankcard associations require written contracts between acquirers and the ISO/MSP. Bankcard associations have specific guidelines relating to contract provisions, functions controlled by the acquiring bank, accessibility to procedural audits, and record keeping requirements. The written contracts should clearly set out the responsibilities of each party, compensation and liability arrangements, allowable uses of the acquiring bank's name, and reasons the contract can be terminated. A bank counsel who is familiar with the specialized nature of merchant processing should review all contracts.

---

[4] Some services provided to national banks by service providers are examined by the Federal Financial Institutions Examinations Council (FFIEC) member agencies. Regulatory examination reports, which are only available to client financial institutions of the service provider, may contain information regarding a service provider's operations. However, regulatory reports are not a substitute for a bank's due diligence, audit, or oversight of the service provider.

Onsite Inspections and Audits

Management should periodically conduct onsite inspections and audits of the third-party organizations. Audit reports should be generated, and the third-party management should be required to respond to identified issues. If the third party is required to have specialized audits (e.g., audits according to Statement of Auditing Standards No. 70) or if it elects to have such audits, management should obtain and review the audits.

Contingency Planning

Acquiring banks must also ensure that the third-party processor and network providers have contingency plans in place to continue operations in the event of a disaster. If an ISO/MSP is providing the backroom operations, the bank also should ensure that the ISO/MSP has a contingency plan. The examiner should determine whether the bank has requested and reviewed contingency plans. The merchant processing examination should include IT examiners to the extent needed to review the adequacy of the contingency plan, as well as the bank's in-house data processing systems for merchant processing.

Loans to Third-party Organizations

Banks must fully understand the total risk exposure when lending to third-party organizations that perform services for the bank. The lending relationship creates a potential conflict of interest and increases the bank's overall credit risk. The risk exposure to the bank is not only the loans but also the contingent liability from merchant processing activities by the third party conducted through the bank's BIN/ICA number. Lending to a third-party organization, such as for working capital, can result in a bank failing to take appropriate action against the third party when problems are identified. For example, the bank may not want to stop processing for the ISO/MSP because it may jeopardize repayment of the bank's loan. As a result, management continues with a problem relationship, which may increase the problems and subsequent losses.

Examination Procedures

These examination procedures include general procedures and agent bank procedures. If the bank being examined offers merchant processing as an agent bank, refer to the agent bank procedures.

General Procedures

Objective: To set the scope of the merchant processing examination and assess the quantity of risk and quality of risk management.

1. Review the following documents to identify any previous problems that require follow-up. Consider:

   • Previous examination findings relating to merchant processing and management's response to those findings.
   • Work performed by internal/external auditors and credit examiners including reports issued and management's response to significant deficiencies.
   • Supervisory strategy and the scope memorandum issued by the bank's examiner-in-charge (EIC).
   • Working papers from the previous examination.

2. Obtain and review management information related to the supervision of merchant processing activities. Consider:

   ☐ The bank's current strategic plan and any other formal plans which relate to merchant processing operations.
   ☐ An organization chart including each functional area.
   ☐ Copies of formal job descriptions for all principals of the merchant processing operation.
   ☐ Resumes detailing experience of principals in the department.
   ☐ Copies of management compensation programs, including incentive plans.

☐ Copies of the two most recent monthly management reports provided to the board of directors for merchant processing operations.

☐ Copies of all internal and external audit reports issued since the last examination, with any response from management.

☐ New merchant report for the previous three months.

☐ A list of board and executive or senior management committees that supervise merchant processing operations, including a list of members and copies of minutes documenting those meetings since the last examination.

☐ The budget for the merchant processing area at the beginning of the year, and budget revisions as of the examination date.

☐ Report on the bank's top 50 merchants by volume.

☐ Copies of Visa, MasterCard, or other applicable association standards and copies of all correspondence from these organizations since last examination.

☐ Copies of marketing plans for the merchant processing operation overall and by product.

☐ Copies of merchant processing policies and procedures.

☐ A profitability report for the department for the most recent year-end and year-to-date and profitability reports by segment.

☐ A list of all insider-related merchants who are customers.

☐ Any management reports on merchants' credit risk.

☐ Daily fraud monitoring reports.

☐ Fraud loss and credit loss history.

☐ Chargeback aging report, chargeback ratio and trend reports.

☐ Name and address of agent banks, and the volumes of business done by the merchants they referred.

☐ List of third parties by name and address and description of service provided.

3.   Identify, during early discussion with management,

• Any changes in business activities (e.g., growth, target market, and products).

• How management supervises merchant processing operations.

- Any significant changes in policies, practices, personnel, and controls.
- Any internal or external factors that could affect merchant processing operations.

4. Using the findings from performing the preceding procedures and from discussions with the bank EIC and other appropriate supervisors, set the examination's scope. Set the examination's objectives. **From the following examination procedures, internal control questions, and verification procedures, select the ones necessary to meet those objectives. Note: Examinations seldom require all steps.**

5. As examination procedures are performed, test for compliance with established policies, procedures, internal controls (the bank should have appropriate controls), OCC regulations, and OCC issuances. Identify any area with inadequate supervision or undue risk.

Procedures: Quantity of Risk

Conclusion: The quantity of risk is (low, moderate, or high)

Objective: To determine the quantity of risk in merchant processing activities.

Management

1. Review the bank's strategic plan and determine whether management's plans for the department are clear and represent the current direction of the department.

2. Determine whether the bankcard associations have placed restrictive guidelines on the bank. If so, assess management's corrective action plan. Restrictions may include requiring a collateral pledge, maintaining higher levels of capital, or prohibiting the bank from signing certain types of merchants.

3. For issues that remain uncorrected, determine whether the board or its audit committee has adopted a corrective action plan.

4. Obtain, through discussion with the merchant manager, information about the overall portfolio, management information systems (MIS), and policies. Significant changes from the prior examination should be reviewed to understand how the changes have affected the portfolio's risk profile.

5. Evaluate any new programs the bank is pursuing and what effect the programs may have on the merchant operation.

6. Determine whether the bank has acquired any merchant portfolios since the previous examination. If so, determine:

    *   The thoroughness of the due diligence review performed by management prior to the purchase.

- The quality of the portfolio as determined by the chargeback rate and loss history.
- Number of accounts and breakdown of merchant accounts by industry (using standard industry code).
- Whether reserve accounts or certificates of deposit (CDs) are pledged against the merchant accounts.
- Whether the purchase was approved by senior management or the board of directors according to bank policy.

7. Determine the volume of transactions being processed in relation to the bank's Tier 1 capital, in aggregate and for transactions deemed high risk.

8. Determine the risk profile of the portfolio. Evaluate the methods the bank uses to rate the risk in its merchant accounts. **Perform verification procedures, if needed, to determine the nature and activities of the merchants and to test the bank's risk assessment.**

Underwriting

1. Evaluate the bank's policy for approving new merchant accounts. Determine whether it addresses the following issues:

- Types of merchants for which the bank does not want to provide merchant processing services (prohibited and restricted lists).
- Documentation requirements for merchant files.
- Underwriting guidelines for merchant accounts.
- Termination procedures for merchant accounts.
- What derogatory information is acceptable on credit reports.
- Criteria for approving processing for additional merchant locations.
- Who in the bank is responsible for approving merchants.
- Handling of exceptions to the merchant approval policy.
- Process for reviewing information collected by ISOs/MSPs.

Chargebacks

1. Review the trend in the volume and aging of chargebacks.

2. Investigate significant trends in both the volume and age of chargebacks:

    *   Discuss with management any merchants who are generating significant chargebacks.
    *   Instruct the bank to charge off any chargebacks aged over 90 days (association rules allow exceeding 90 days in limited circumstances).

3. Determine whether the bank has suffered any significant losses from merchant chargebacks over the past several years.

Settlement

1. Review management's analysis of risk if the bank uses a BIN or ICA number (whether it owns the number or not).

Agent Bank Programs

1. Review the bank's agent bank programs and determine the level of liability assumed by the acquirer.

2. Obtain a report that shows merchant volume per agent bank. Review agent banks that have a significant volume of transactions.

3. Review a sample of agent bank files. Evaluate whether the information in the files is adequate and check for compliance with policy.

Pricing

1. Review the bank's pricing policies and evaluate the bank's pricing methods. If the bank offers reduced discount rates based on other existing banking relationships, evaluate the risks and rewards.

2. Review management's analysis of whether individual merchants are profitable for the bank. Investigate reasons for low profitability or losses.

3. Obtain discount rates from the merchant file review worksheet and compare actual pricing against the pricing policy.

4. Determine which personnel have the authority to set pricing variables and how management monitors the pricing process.

5. Coordinate with the examiner reviewing third-party organizations to determine other pricing programs used. Determine whether pricing is tied to the sale or lease of equipment or other services.

Profitability

1. Review the department's profitability statements. Evaluate major costs and fee income items in relation to overall profitability. Determine the impact of chargeback and fraud losses on profitability.

Third-party Organizations

1. Determine what third-party organizations the acquiring bank uses for merchant processing services.

2. Obtain a report that shows merchant sales volume per ISO. Review ISOs that have significant volume or growth.

3. Determine whether contracts are on file for each third-party organization.

4. Evaluate whether the bank periodically reviews its third-party servicers. Information available may include financial statements, third-party operational reviews, disaster contingency plans, and reports of bank regulatory agencies.

5. Review major contracts to assess the following information:

- Terms specifying financial compensation, payment arrangements, and price changes.
- Provisions prohibiting the third party from assigning the agreement to any other party.
- Frequency and means of communication and monitoring activities of each party.
- Specific work to be performed by the third-party servicer.
- Whether the contract provides for the confidential treatment of records.
- Record keeping requirements each party must maintain and whether the other party has access to these records.
- Responsibility for audits and whether the acquirer has the right to audit the third-party organization.
- Notification requirements of system changes that could affect procedures and reports.
- Type and frequency of financial information the third party will provide.
- Whether contractual penalties for terminating the contract seem reasonable.

6. Review a sample of ISO/MSP contracts for the appropriate provisions. In addition to general contract provisions, the contracts should:

- Tie fees to performance (e.g., number of merchants, volume of sales transactions, chargeback activity).
- Define responsibilities for fraud and chargeback losses.
- Require security deposits from the ISO/MSP if its financial condition is weak or the quality of the merchants it solicits on behalf of the bank is poor.
- Include remedies to protect the bank if the ISO/MSP fails to perform (including indemnity, early termination rights, delayed payment of residuals).
- State the criteria for accepting merchants.
- Specify that the bank owns the merchant relationships.
- Control the future use and solicitation of merchants.

- Define the allowable use of the bank's and the ISO/MSP's name, trade name, and logo.
- Permit bank employees to conduct onsite inspections of the ISO/MSP.
- Warrant that all federal consumer laws and bankcard association rules are to be followed.

7. Review a sample of ISO/MSP credit files and check for compliance with policy. At a minimum, the files should contain:

- An analysis of the current financial statement of the principals and the ISO/MSP. The type of financial statement should correlate to the size of the company.
- A document detailing a bank employee's onsite inspection of the ISO/MSP.
- Evidence that bank and trade references have been verified.
- A credit report on the principals of the ISO/MSP.
- A criminal check on the principals of the ISO/MSP.

8. Determine whether ISO/MSP reserve accounts are consistent with the condition of the company and volume of business generated.

9. List third-party processors that have provided contingency plan information to the bank. Review the bank's analysis of contingency plans to determine adequacy. If an analysis does not exist, review the reasonableness of contingency plans.

10. Determine whether third-party contingency plans are adequately considered in the bank's overall contingency plan.

Procedures: Quality of Risk Management

Conclusion: The quality of risk management is (strong, satisfactory, weak)

Policies

Conclusion: The board (has/has not) established effective policies and standards for merchant processing.

Objective: To determine whether the board of directors has adopted policies and standards for merchant processing that are consistent with safe and sound banking practices and appropriate to the scope of its operations.

Management

1. Determine what policies have been approved by the board of directors for merchant processing.

2. Evaluate the overall adequacy of written policies using examiner findings in each of the areas.

3. Determine whether the board evaluates policies for changing market and business conditions at least annually.

Chargebacks

1. Determine whether the bank has a policy for charging off stale chargebacks (generally 90 days) and assess the policy's appropriateness.

Agent Bank Programs

1. Determine whether the acquirer has a policy that addresses agent banks for which the acquirer provides service. Does the policy address:

- Criteria for accepting agent banks?
- An agent bank's merchant underwriting?
- Policy exceptions?
- An agent bank's liability?
- Periodic reviews?

Third-party Organizations

1. Determine whether the board has adopted a policy for underwriting new independent sales organizations or member service providers (ISOs/MSPs). If so, determine whether the policy states that:

- The ISO/MSP must provide the acquiring bank certain financial information (the policy should stipulate its type and timing).
- An experienced commercial credit officer must review the periodic financial statements of the ISO/MSP.
- Management must review the depth and experience of the ISO/MSP management.
- The bank must perform required background checks, and the checks should determine whether any ISO/MSP or its principals have criminal records.
- The bank must obtain required bank and trade references on all ISOs/MSPs and their principals.
- The ISO/MSP must maintain specific reserve accounts to absorb losses from merchant chargebacks or other damages if the organization is financially liable for losses.

Processes

Conclusion: Management and the board (have/have not) established effective processes for merchant processing.

Objective: To determine whether processes, including internal controls, are adequate and consistent with sound merchant processing practices.

Underwriting

1. Evaluate the bank's procedures for ensuring compliance with the merchant approval policy.

2. Determine how the bank documents and monitors performance of exceptions to the merchant approval policy. Evaluate the practices for waiving documentation requirements.

3. Determine whether the bank has a written agreement with each merchant and whether the agreement contains the following information:

    *   The fees to be charged to the merchant.
    *   The requirements the merchant must meet at the point of sale.
    *   Required information for chargebacks.
    *   A merchant's redress if the agreement is terminated or suspended.
    *   Whether the merchant must notify the bank of a change in ownership.
    *   Whether the merchant is subject to continuing review by the bank or a designated third party.
    *   A statement requiring the merchant to follow bankcard association rules.
    *   Whether the merchant assumes liability for problems associated with insecure transmission of credit card data and storage of customer information for Internet merchants.

4. Select a representative sample of recently approved merchant files (for example, within the last 90 days). The sample should include merchants that the bank obtains directly, through ISOs/MSPs, and through agent banks. If possible, the sample of merchants obtained directly by the bank should include a sample of merchants by size and industry. Review the sample of merchant files for compliance with the policy.

5. Summarize the results of the merchant file review. Determine whether the level of exceptions is reasonable in view of board-approved policies.

6. In evaluating the bank's ongoing review of merchant accounts, determine:

   • The type or size of merchant accounts eligible for review.
   • The frequency of the review.
   • Whether the review is coordinated with the commercial loan department.
   • The type and timing of the financial information the bank asks merchants to provide.
   • The performance factors included in the review (e.g., level and trends in transactions, returns, and chargebacks).

7. Evaluate how the bank determines while underwriting when to set up a merchant reserve or holdback. If reserves are established, how frequently are they reviewed?

Chargeback Systems

1. Evaluate the adequacy of the chargeback system. Determine whether the system is automated or manual and whether it can:

   • Quantify outstanding chargebacks and their age.
   • Prioritize research into chargebacks.
   • Measure the efficiency of the chargeback process.

2. Determine how the bank evaluates the adequacy of its chargeback systems.

3. Inquire how the bank plans for contingencies, such as large merchant bankruptcies, which can generate a large volume of chargebacks.

4. Describe how management assigns chargeback work to employees, such as by age, reason code, or merchant.

5. Review the bank's procedures for establishing merchant-funded chargeback reserves on high chargeback merchants. Determine whether current practices sufficiently protect the bank from exposure to chargeback loss.

6. If the bank is not adequately protected from chargeback losses, determine whether the bank needs a bank-funded general reserve or additional capital support.

7. Evaluate the collection of chargeback losses and uncollected fees.

Settlement

1. Review the settlement flow chart. Identify all parties involved, each party's responsibility, and the estimated time that it takes funds and transaction data to flow from party to party during the settlement process.

2. If the bank does not pay merchants the same day it receives credit from issuers, assess management's procedures to keep the funds segregated and liquid.

Profit Analysis

1. Review the bank's budgeting process for its merchant business and investigate the budget's significant variances from actual performance. Determine whether the department is expected to meet this year's budget and, if not, why not.

2. Evaluate the MIS used in determining the department's profitability.

3. Determine how management arrives at cost figures, that is, whether it uses actual or estimated costs, and whether the methodology is appropriate.

Third-party Organizations

1. Determine the monitoring levels and reasonableness of ISO/MSP system access. All system changes should have prior approval of a bank employee.

Personnel

Conclusion: Management (does/does not) have the skills and knowledge necessary to manage the risk inherent in merchant processing.

Objective: To determine management's ability to conduct merchant processing in a safe and sound manner.

Management

1. Review the resumes of the principals in the merchant processing department. Determine whether the staff has adequate experience in merchant processing and is adequately trained.

2. Review the organizational chart for the department to determine what, if any, other responsibilities the merchant manager has within the bank. Determine whether the organizational structure is appropriate.

3. Determine what committees, if any, are involved in the merchant processing operation. Review the committee's minutes for pertinent information. Determine whether the committee structures, if any, are appropriate.

Staffing Levels

1. Determine whether current staffing levels fit the bank's short-term and long-term requirements. Determine whether:

- Staffing levels are adequate to the volume of merchant accounts, the number of applications reviewed daily, processing needs, and the need to oversee third parties.
- Personnel reviewing merchant applications are qualified.
- Staffing levels are sufficient to handle resolution of chargebacks within bankcard association time frames.
- Staffing levels are sufficient to investigate daily fraud exception reports in a timely manner.
- Staff turnover seems high.

Audit

1. Determine the internal/external auditor's knowledge of the merchant processing area and whether the auditor's knowledge is adequate to perform effective reviews.

Controls

Conclusion: Management and the board (have/have not) implemented effective control systems.

Objective: To determine whether internal/external audit, management information systems, and any other control systems should enable the bank to manage merchant processing adequately.

Management

1. Assess the adequacy of the overall management information systems (MIS).

   - Review the MIS reports routinely used by management and determine whether they adequately inform management of the department's condition.
   - Review reports to the board and determine whether the information the directors receive is meaningful and complete. At a minimum, reports should include information for each

portfolio segment including agent bank and ISO portfolios. Information should include sales volumes, merchant types, profitability chargeback activity, and fraud activity.

Perform verification procedures if the reports and trial balances contain unusual information or information that cannot be readily explained.

Audit

1.   Review the scope and frequency of the internal audit. Determine whether it addresses all operational areas.

2.   Determine whether the internal audit reviews major services provided by third-party organizations.

Fraud

1.   Determine whether the scope and frequency of fraud reviews are adequate. Assess how analysts prioritize exceptions and whether certain potentially suspicious transactions are processed through more sophisticated systems (e.g., scoring and other databases).

2.   Determine whether management has established parameters for monitoring Internet transactions.

3.   Determine how the bank establishes parameters for exceptions.

4.   Determine who in the bank can set fraud parameters and what documentation is required to change the parameters.

5.   Determine the frequency with which management updates a merchant's historical sales volume.

6. Determine the bank's course of action when it detects suspicious activity. (Does the bank delay settlement, establish merchant funded reserves, or file a Suspicious Activity Report, for example?)

7. Review the acquiring bank's controls over delaying settlement funds to determine whether they comply with bankcard association regulations.

8. Review any parameters for exceptions that are available to the acquirer but not presently in use. Commonly used parameters are:

    - Large average ticket size.
    - Large daily or weekly volume.
    - Keyed rather than swiped transactions.
    - Multiple tickets in the same dollar amount.
    - Multiple use of same cardholder number.
    - High chargeback activity.
    - Excessive return volumes.
    - Declined authorizations.
    - Authorizations not matched to sales and vice versa.
    - Transactions from inactive or closed accounts.

9. If a neural network is used, review management's rationale for the parameters that have been set.

Third-party Organizations

1. Review the merchant department's procedures for monitoring the third party's quality control and compliance with the contract. Monitoring for quality control should (as applicable):

    - Ensure that the ISO/MSP is properly registered with the bankcard associations.
    - Determine the adequacy of the ISO/MSPs' written operating procedures.
    - Ensure that the bank approves all ISO/MSPs' training material, marketing material, and discount and fee schedules.

- Verify that ISO/MSP sales people meet the bank's criteria for criminal and credit checks.
- Sample merchants solicited by the ISO/MSP for compliance with policies.
- Compare approval and rejection rates with department projections.
- Review the quality of customer service activities.
- Review how the bank and the ISO/MSP resolve merchant complaints.
- Evaluate the timeliness of chargeback processing and appropriateness of decisions.
- Evaluate how decisions were made on exceptions that could affect fraud monitoring.
- Determine the adequacy of merchant and third-party reserve accounts, if appropriate.
- Assess compliance with bankcard association regulations.

2. Determine whether the management of the merchant department requires the third party to adopt a written action plan to correct deficiencies when results fall below bank standards.

3. Review the bank's MIS used to monitor activities of the ISO/MSP.

Agent Bank: Examination Procedures

General Agent Bank Procedures

Objective: To determine the quantity of risk and quality of risk management of merchant processing activities at an agent bank. These procedures will typically be used at smaller community banks that are the agent banks of an acquirer. These procedures should not be used to evaluate an acquirer's agent bank program.

1. Obtain the following for all agent bank arrangements:

    ☐   The agent bank agreement.

2. For agent banks with liability obtain:

    ☐   Monthly volume and profitability reports from the acquiring bank.
    ☐   Reports on monitoring chargebacks and fraud.
    ☐   Merchant processing policies.

Agent Bank Procedures: Quantity of Risk

Conclusion: The quantity of risk is (low, moderate, or high).

Objective: To determine the quantity of risk of an agent bank's merchant processing activities.

1. Review the agent bank agreement to ensure that it:

    - Is current and in writing.
    - Defines the party responsible for fraud and chargeback losses.
    - Identifies who is responsible for underwriting new merchants.
    - Identifies who will price the merchant account.
    - Specifies the income the agent will receive.
    - Contains confidentiality provisions.
    - Defines the sharing of BIN/ICA, if applicable.

2. By reviewing the agent bank agreement, determine whether the bank is acting only as a referral bank and has **no** liability for fraud and/or chargeback losses.

3. Determine whether the referral/agent bank has signed any indemnification agreements on individual merchant accounts that the acquiring bank would have otherwise denied. If not, no further work is recommended for referral banks. If so, review a sample of these accounts to determine whether the referral bank took on excessive risk in signing these merchants.

    Complete the remaining procedures if the bank retains loss liability.

4. Document the volume of merchant transactions the agent bank has processed for the prior year and year-to-date.

5. Determine the source and composition of the bank's merchant portfolio.

6.	Determine whether the merchant portfolio has concentration risk by industry, merchant segment, or individual merchant that could adversely affect the bank.

7.	Determine whether the bank maintains any merchant holdback reserves to mitigate risk.

8.	Determine whether the bank performs its own underwriting. If so, review a sample of new merchant accounts to determine compliance with underwriting standards.

9.	Determine whether the bank has incurred any significant chargeback or fraud losses in the past year.

10.	If the bank sets pricing variables, determine what method is used (e.g., matrix, formula, or pricing model). Determine whether:

	•	The pricing system takes into account all of the bank's costs.
	•	Pricing on the bank's largest merchant accounts (e.g., top 10) is profitable.

11.	Analyze profitability by reviewing income statements and/or profitability reports on the bank's merchant activity.

12.	Determine whether the acquiring bank or the agent bank shares a BIN/ICA with other banks. If so, determine who is responsible for fraud and chargeback losses experienced by any other bank processing under the BIN/ICA.

Agent Bank Procedures: Quality of Risk Management

Conclusion: The quality of risk management is (strong, satisfactory, or weak).

Policies

Conclusion: The board (has/has not) established effective policies and standards governing merchant processing activities at an agent bank.

Objective: To determine whether the board of directors has adopted policies and standards for merchant processing at an agent bank that are consistent with safe and sound banking practices and appropriate to the scope of its operations.

1. If the bank has a significant volume of merchant activity in relation to its capital base, determine whether the bank has adequate policies in place to control risks. Determine whether:

    •   The policy addresses underwriting standards (customers vs. non-customers), pricing, liability provisions, and management and board reporting.
    •   The board has established policies on concentration limits.
    •   The policy states who is authorized to approve merchants and outlines procedures for approving exceptions.

Processes

Conclusion: Management and the board (have/have not) established effective processes relating to merchant processing activities at an agent bank.

Objective: To determine whether processes, including internal controls, are adequate and consistent with merchant processing practices.

1. Determine the adequacy of the agent bank's systems for monitoring the credit risk of its largest merchants. Determine whether the agent relies on the acquiring bank to conduct periodic reviews.

2. Determine types and adequacy of information on merchant chargebacks and on the bank's monitoring for fraud.

Personnel

Conclusion: Management (does/does not) have the skills and knowledge necessary to manage the risk inherent in merchant processing activities at an agent bank.

Objective: To determine management's ability to conduct an agent bank's merchant processing activities in a safe and sound manner.

1. Determine management's understanding of merchant processing activities (e.g., ability to understand liability and responsibilities under the agent bank agreement).

2. Determine who has the authority to price a merchant account outside the pricing guidelines. Select a sample of merchant accounts to determine whether exceptions were properly approved.

3. Assess the adequacy of customer support provided to the agent by the acquirer under the terms of the agent bank agreement. For example, determine whether customer support includes the following services:

    - Periodic management reports on portfolio volume and activity.
    - Notification of chargeback volumes and actual losses from chargebacks and fraud.
    - An annual risk profile.
    - Training.

Controls

Conclusion: Management and the board (have/have not) implemented effective control systems for merchant processing activities at an agent bank.

Objective: To determine the adequacy of internal/external audit, management information systems, and any other control systems as they relate to merchant processing activities at an agent bank.

1.   Assess whether adequate controls are in place to identify and measure the bank's risk (e.g., reporting and portfolio analysis).

2.   Evaluate the internal audit program to ensure that its reviews are commensurate with the volume and quantity of risk in the program.

Conclusions

This "Conclusions" section applies to the general procedures and the agent bank procedures.

Objective: To determine overall conclusions and communicate examination findings regarding the quality of risk and risk management systems in merchant processing activities.

Objective: To initiate corrective action when policies, practices, procedures, or internal controls are deficient or when violations of law, rulings, or regulations have been noted.

1. Prepare a memorandum to the EIC or examiner assigned loan portfolio management regarding:

   - The quality of the department's management.
   - Quantity of risk. Consider:
     - Credit quality and collectibility of the merchant accounts, as well as losses.
     - Volume and type of merchants.
     - Compliance with established guidelines, including bankcard association operating regulations.
     - Compliance with applicable laws, rulings, and regulations.
   - Quality of risk management. Consider:
     - Adequacy of policies.
     - Adequacy of processes, including planning.
     - Management's ability to conduct merchant processing activities in a safe and sound manner.
     - Adequacy of control systems, including audit and management information systems.

- Any concerns or recommendations regarding condition of department including:
  - Root causes of problems.
  - Factors contributing to any less than satisfactory conditions.
- Adverse trends within the merchant processing department.
- The accuracy and completeness of the bank's MIS reports.
- Internal control deficiencies or exceptions.
- The adequacy of departmental planning, including projected growth areas.
- Violations of laws, rulings, and regulations.
- Management's strategies to correct noted deficiencies.

2. Determine the impact on aggregate risk and the direction of risk from any applicable risks identified while performing the above procedures. Examiners should refer to guidance provided under the OCC's Large Bank and Community Bank risk assessment programs.

- Risk Categories: Credit, Transaction, Liquidity, Compliance, Reputation, and Strategic
- Risk Conclusions: High, Moderate, or Low
- Risk Direction: Increasing, Stable, or Declining

3. Determine, in consultation with the EIC, whether the risks identified are significant enough to bring them to the board's attention in the report of examination. If so, prepare items under the heading "Matters Requiring Attention":

- MRA should cover practices that:
  - Deviate from sound fundamental principles and are likely to result in financial deterioration if not addressed.
  - Result in substantive noncompliance with laws.
- MRA should discuss:
  - Causes of the problem.
  - Consequences of inaction.
  - Management's commitment to corrective action.
  - The time frame and person(s) responsible for corrective action.

4   Discuss findings with management, including conclusions regarding applicable risks.

5.   As appropriate, include a comment on merchant processing in the report of examination.

6.   Provide either the examiner assigned LPM or the bank EIC with a memorandum specifically stating what the OCC should do in the future to effectively supervise merchant processing activities. Include supervisory objectives, timing of activities, staffing requirements, and an estimate of workdays required.

7.   Prepare a memorandum or update the work program with any information that will facilitate future examinations.

8.   Update the ongoing supervisory record and any applicable report of examination schedules or tables.

9.   Complete the EV indicators for merchant processing when available.

10.   Organize and reference working papers in accordance with OCC guidance.

Internal Control Questionnaire

Policies and Procedures

1. Has the board of directors adopted a written policy on merchant processing that:

    *   Establishes clear lines of authority and responsibility?
    *   Identifies the risks the bank is willing to accept as well as limits the amount of those risks?
    *   Limits the individual and aggregate volume of the bank's merchant activity?
    *   Provides for adequate and knowledgeable staff?
    *   Requires written contracts between all third parties?
    *   Establishes criteria for the acceptance of merchants?
    *   Requires the development of procedures to monitor the activity of each merchant?
    *   Establishes when merchant reserve (holdback) accounts are appropriate?
    *   Establishes risk-based guidelines for the periodic review of merchant creditworthiness?
    *   Develops criteria for contracting with any ISO to act as agent for the bank?
    *   Requires the development of adequate MIS systems to keep management and the board informed of the program's condition?
    *   Requires that a comprehensive procedure manual be developed to guide officers and employees in administering the program?
    *   Establishes guidelines for handling exceptions to policy?
    *   Establishes guidelines for the acceptance of agent banks?
    *   Requires review of all contracts and applications by legal counsel familiar with merchant processing?

2. Are merchant processing policies and objectives reviewed at least annually to determine their compatibility with current market conditions and the bank's strategic plan?

3. Is the procedures manual comprehensive and current and does it provide for:

   - Establishing new business?
   - Monitoring existing business?
   - Dealing with ISOs/MSPs?
   - Handling complaints with merchants?
   - Conducting settlement procedures — both ACH and wire transfer?
   - Processing merchant retrievals and chargebacks?
   - Addressing fraud monitoring and reporting?
   - Training new personnel?

Management and Board Supervision

1. Does the merchant processing department have an organizational chart?

2. Does the manager of the merchant operations have merchant processing experience?

3. Are the reports received by the board and management appropriate and timely?

4. Have appropriate backup managers or staff been trained to handle critical areas?

5. Does the staffing keep pace with the volume of merchant applications received daily?

6. Is staff turnover high?

7. Do MIS reports include information on:

- Concentrations by type of industry?
- Geographic distribution of merchants?
- High-volume merchants?
- Attrition?
- Number of active merchant accounts?
- Aggregate sales volume for the month and year?
- Number of transactions for the month and year?
- Average discount rate of the portfolio?
- Average per unit cost?
- Whether the bank profits from each merchant (the report should show which merchants are not profitable for the bank)?
- Chargebacks as a percentage of sales?
- New merchants?
- Audit deficiency tracking?

8. Has the board adopted a strategic plan for the department?

9. Is the board adequately informed about merchant processing activities?

10. Is a separate pro-forma budget prepared for the department?

11. Has the board reviewed the bonding needs of the department?

12. Does the bank have an effective project management function to ensure timely implementation of new products and systems?

13. Do the personnel reviewing funding needs for the bank consider the impact of merchant processing?

Audit Coverage

1. Does the merchant processing department receive audit coverage?

2.   Is the internal/external auditor knowledgeable about merchant processing?

3.   Do audit reports, for both the bank and third parties, require written management responses to significant deficiencies?

4.   Do merchant processing audits:

-   Address all operational areas?
-   Verify that the board has approved risk limits, such as processing volume, types of merchants, geographic restrictions, and concentrations by industry and large merchants?
-   Test compliance with policy?
-   Determine compliance with departmental operating procedures?
-   Ensure that the department has adequate processes to comply with bankcard association regulations?
-   Assess compliance with written contracts?
-   Test adherence to approval authorities delegated to department employees?
-   Verify that the bank's contingency planning coordinator periodically reviews the adequacy of each third party's disaster recovery plan?
-   Validate the accuracy of cost accounting controls in determining the effectiveness of pricing and profitability analyses?
-   Ensure that changes in discount rates and fees are authorized by senior department management?
-   Ensure that departmental staff periodically review third-party deposit accounts for unusual activity?
-   Validate the accuracy and controls involved for the bank's merchant and ISO reserves?
-   Determine the appropriate usage and reconciliation of balance sheet accounts?
-   Determine that management appropriately accounts for stale balance sheet items?
-   Assess overall risk in the area?

5.   Does the bank require that all ISOs/MSPs have operational audits?

Approving Merchants

1.   Does the policy on approving merchants provide for clear and measurable underwriting standards for merchants?

2.   Does the bank require merchant applications to be in writing?

3.   Does the bank perform inspections or use other types of verifications for all merchants?

4.   Are the inspections and verifications documented?

5.   Are statements of previous merchant activity required for all new merchant applications?

6.   Does the policy address:

- Desirable vs. undesirable merchants?
- Documentation requirements for each merchant's file?
- Who is authorized to approve merchants?
- Merchant underwriting guidelines?
- Merchant termination procedures?
- Handling exceptions to the merchant approval policy?
- Type and timing of financial information to be provided by merchants?

7.   Does the person reviewing merchant applications have credit experience?

8.   Are the financial statements of all large merchants reviewed by a person (or committee) with extensive commercial loan experience?

9.   Are the financial statements of all large merchants reviewed at least annually?

10. Does the bank require reserves against the accounts of high-risk merchants or those of merchants incurring a significant amount of chargebacks?

11. Are merchant reserve accounts kept separate from their operating accounts and not commingled with other merchant reserve accounts?

Settlement Process

1. If processing failure occurs at any point, is the bank obligated to fund merchant sales?

2. Does the bank settle directly with the merchant?

3. Are written agreements in place for parties involved in the settlement process?

4. Are contracts with network vendors made with the acquirer rather than ISOs/MSPs?

5. Are all merchant and ISO/MSP funds held as chargeback or loss reserves placed in individual deposit accounts, separate from settlement proceeds?

6. Is access to merchant and ISO reserve accounts restricted to bank personnel?

7. Are adequate procedures followed to refund merchant and ISO/MSP reserves according to the terms in the merchant agreement?

8. When merchant reserves cannot be successfully refunded, do procedures ensure compliance with abandoned property and state escheat laws?

9. Can the bank hold merchant funds pending the resolution of suspected fraudulent activity?

10. Are payments to merchants made with collected settlement funds (funds for sales received from the issuer via the associations)?

11. Are merchant and ISO accounts reviewed for suspicious activity?

12. Have contingency plans been developed and reviewed for all parties involved in the settlement process?

13. If ISOs perform accounting and servicing functions, have contingency plans been developed to cover their services?

14. Are there procedures to ensure the accuracy of ACH and wire transfer files, whether originated at the bank or by a third-party processor?

15. Are there controls for handling rejected ACH and wire transfer items?

16. Has management obtained third-party reviews and regulatory examination reports of its processors?

Chargeback Processing

1. Are policies and procedures in place for chargeback processing?

2. Can the bank generate reports on:

   • Daily chargeback activity?
   • Status and aging of chargebacks?
   • Exception reports on merchants experiencing unusual chargeback activity?

3. Are losses from merchant chargebacks clearly identified on the general ledger as noninterest expense?

4. Does the bank debit merchants for chargeback at the same time the bank pays the issuer?

5. Is the staff sufficient to process retrieval requests and chargebacks within the bankcard association's time frames?

Fraud Detection

1. Does the bank have an early warning system to detect a merchant's fraud?

2. Are fraud reports reviewed daily?

3. Are bank employees trained in detecting merchant fraud?

4. Are exception parameters for fraud reports tailored to each merchant?

5. Do exception reports screen for:

- Significant variances from average ticket size?
- Significant variances in daily and weekly volume?
- Multiple tickets in the same dollar amount?
- Multiple use of same cardholder number?
- Keyed rather than swiped transactions?
- Transactions from inactive or closed accounts?
- A high rate of chargebacks?
- Authorizations not matched to sales, and vice versa?
- Authorization declines?
- Excessive returns relative to sales?

6. Does the bank have a process to file Suspicious Activity Reports (SARs) with the Financial Crimes Enforcement Network (FinCEN) in accordance with 12 CFR 21.11?

7. Does management have an effective process to respond to bankcard association reports in a timely manner?

8.	Are fraud losses reported on the Consolidated Report of Income as noninterest expenses?

9.	Does management perform post mortem analysis of fraud losses?

Agent Banks

1.	Are agent bank agreements in writing?

2.	Are agent banks informed of their financial liability for a merchant's fraud and/or chargeback losses?

3.	Are merchants obtained through agent banks subject to the same underwriting standards as direct or ISO merchants?

4.	Does the bank routinely obtain and review financial information on agent banks?

5.	Are separate files maintained for each agent bank?

6.	Are proper approval authorities obtained for each agent bank?

7.	Does the policy on selecting agent banks address:

- The bank's financial condition?
- Early termination of the relationship with the agent bank if unsafe and unsound activities are suspected?
- Periodic financial review of agent banks with high-volume or high-risk merchants?

Third-Party Organizations

1.	Has the bank registered all ISO/MSP with bankcard associations?

2. Does the bank periodically analyze or review the finances of all third-party organizations?

3. Does the bank perform periodic onsite inspections of all bank ISOs/MSPs?

4. Does the bank review and approve all promotional material used by ISOs/MSPs?

5. Does the bank attend sales training sessions for ISO/MSP salespeople?

6. Does the bank require that each ISO/MSP have operational audits?

Pricing

1. Does the bank's pricing policy address:

   - Minimum discount rates?
   - Pricing methods used, such as standard matrix or bid models?
   - Handling exceptions to the pricing policy?
   - Which personnel, including ISO/MSP salespeople, have the authority to price merchants?
   - Monitoring whether merchants are profitable for the bank?
   - Repricing guidelines?
   - Documentation requirements for discount rate reviews?

2. Does the bank's pricing system address:

   - Overhead costs, including employee costs, educational and training costs, occupancy costs?
   - Internal and external processing costs, including cost of computer hardware, software, and phone lines?
   - Interchange fees?
   - Bankcard association assessments?
   - Revenue for providing float to the clearing process?

- Chargeback costs?
- Desired profit margins?
- Insurance and bonding needs?
- Loss history and the risk of future loss?

3. Does the bank track the date the merchants were last repriced?

4. Does the bank ensure that all outlets related to a merchant account are priced consistently?

5. Can the bank determine whether individual merchants are profitable for the bank?

Department Profitability

1. Does the department have a separate financial statement from the others areas in the bank?

2. Does the merchant department's profitability statements include all direct and overhead costs including corporate allocations?

3. Does the department have an approved budget, and, if so, does the budget seem realistic?

4. Are significant variances from the budget explained?

5. Does the MIS provide information regarding the following:

- Sales volume?
- Total transactions?
- Return on sales?
- Per transaction/unit cost?
- Per transaction/unit income?
- Overhead per merchant?
- Attrition rates?
- Unprofitable merchants?

Credit Card Equipment

1.   For those banks providing point-of-sale equipment to merchants, is access to the inventory limited to authorized personnel?

2.   Are inventory control logs maintained?

Verification Procedures

1. Test the additions to the trial balance(s) and the reconciliation of the trial balance(s) to the controlling subsidiary ledger(s).

2. Using an appropriate sampling technique, select merchants from the reports and:

   - Prepare and mail confirmation forms to merchants (confirm sales volumes as of last statement date).
   - After a reasonable period of time, mail second requests.
   - Follow up on any failures to reply or exceptions and resolve differences.

3. Using the sample from #2, review merchant files and:

   - Examine each agreement with a merchant for completeness and appropriate approval authority.
   - If the agreement requires holdbacks or reserves, compare actual on-deposit holdings against required levels; investigate discrepancies.
   - Check the current discount rate and ensure that it complies with the pricing policy in place at time of approval or repricing.
   - Check application estimates for volume and average ticket size to determine how much they vary from actual performance.
   - Check to determine whether management ran the merchant against Member Alert to Control High-Risk Merchants (MATCH).

4. Obtain or prepare a schedule showing monthly transaction volume, monthly chargeback volume, and all associated monthly revenues and expenses since the last examination:

   - Investigate all significant fluctuations or trends.
   - Determine whether the transaction volumes and chargeback volumes are commensurate with the revenues and expenses.

- Trace revenue and expense transactions to source documents if unusual variances exist.

Appendix A: Portfolio Profile Worksheet

Bank name	
Bank address	
Type of merchant processing (MP) activity (acquirer, agent with or without risk)	
Name of merchant processing contact person	
Phone number of contact person	
Bank Internet address	
Number of employees dedicated to MP activities	#
Number of Visa BINs owned/active	#
Number of MasterCard ICAs owned/active	#
Are any BINs/ICAs shared with another financial institution? (yes or no)	
Sales Volumes Processed	
YTD (/ /)	$
YE prior year 1	$
YE prior year 2	$
Number of transactions - YTD and prior year	#
Average ticket size - YTD and prior year	$
Total number of merchants	#
Number of active merchants	#
Internet sales volume processed	$
Geographic concentration (local, regional, national)	
Three largest merchants by sales volume	1.
(include name and YTD sales volume)	2.
	3.
Current attrition level	%
Niche market (if applicable)	

Processing Systems	
Front-end authorization and capture (major front-end systems used)	
Back-end processing system (in-house or vendor name)	
Chargebacks	
Chargeback monitoring system (in-house or vendor name)	
Chargebacks processed YTD	$
Chargebacks processed YE prior year 1	$
Chargebacks processed YE prior year 2	$
YTD chargeback ratio (dollars)	%
YTD chargeback ratio (number)	%
Fraud Monitoring	
Fraud monitoring system used (in-house or vendor name)	
YTD gross fraud losses	$
Net fraud losses after reimbursement/ Indemnification	$
YE prior year 1 - Gross fraud losses	$
Net fraud losses after reimbursement/ Indemnification	$
YE prior year 2 - Gross fraud losses	$
Net fraud losses after reimbursement/ Indemnification	$
Reserve Volumes	
General merchant reserves	$
Specific merchant reserves	$
ISO reserves	$
ALLL merchant reserves	$

Profitability Information	
Typical retail discount	%
Typical retail per item charge	$
Typical application fee	$
Typical statement fee	$
Typical chargeback fee	$
Equipment Sales (in-house or vendor name)	
Independent Sales Organizations	
Number of ISOs used	#
Association Information	
% Visa sales processed	%
% MasterCard sales processed	%
$ pledged to Visa, if applicable	$
$ pledged to MasterCard, if applicable	$
Is the bank in the Visa High-Risk Acquirer Program? (yes or no)	

Appendix B: Request Letter

Request Letter Enclosure

Please provide copies of the following:

Management and Board Supervision

1. Current organizational chart for the department.

2. Resumes of all principals in the department.

3. Job descriptions of all principal positions.

4. Strategic and business plans and budgets for the department.

5. Two most recent sets of monthly management reports routinely reviewed by management and the board of directors.

6. Report on new merchants or management summaries for the previous three months.

7. Any credit risk management reports of merchant accounts.

8. Report on the bank's top 50 merchants by volume.

9. Concentration reports by industry code, and state or geographic area.

Sales

10. Brief explanation of sales/account acquisition channels.

Underwriting

11. A listing of all insider-related merchant customers.

12. Samples of merchant agreements and applications.

13. List of all merchant reserves.

Profitability

14. Profitability report for the department for the most recent year-end and year-to-date.

15. Fee schedule.

16. Profitability reports by sales segment.

17. An analysis of whether the bank's merchants are profitable for the institution, if available.

18. Report detailing total number of merchants, annual volume of sales, and number of transactions.

19. Listing of the unprofitable accounts.

20. Attrition report for the past year.

Agent Banks

21. Brief summary of agent bank programs offered.

22. Name and address of agent banks, and the volume of merchant processing ascribable to these banks.

23. Sample agent bank agreement.

Third-Party Organizations

24. List of third parties used by name and address and description of service provided.

25. Names and addresses of each ISO/MSP, and number of merchants, sales volume, and number of transactions attributable to each ISO/MSP.

26. List of any loan relationships to third parties including loan terms and amounts.

27. Most recent bank audit report of ISO/MSP activity and ISO/MSP response.

28. Summary of which ISO/MSPs have access to the acquirer's data processing system and the extent of the access (e.g., set-up, chargebacks, or maintenance).

29. List of all ISO reserves.

Settlement

30. A flow chart and brief explanation of the settlement process that illustrates the parties involved and the timing of settlement.

Risk Management

31. Management summary of underwriting exceptions/overrides.

32. Brief description of the fraud monitoring process, the systems and reports used, prioritization of investigations, and staffing involved in the process.

33. Examples of daily fraud monitoring reports.

34. Parameter setting summary for fraud monitoring system.

35. Brief description of the chargeback process, the systems and reports used, prioritization of the research process, and staffing involved in the process.

36. Chargeback aging report, chargeback ratios, and trend analysis.

37. Fraud loss history for the most recent year-end and year-to-date.

38. Credit loss history for the most recent year-end and year-to-date.

39. The last four quarterly monitoring reports for each association (Visa and MasterCard).

40. The bank's analysis of capital with respect to the acquiring operations of the bank.

41. Any additional risk analysis or reports used to evaluate the portfolio apart from daily monitoring reports.

Audit

42. Most recent internal/external audit report and management's response.

Portfolio Acquisitions

43. Listing of any portfolio acquisitions in past 24 months.

44. Due diligence process used for portfolio acquisitions.

45. Management reports used to monitor and manage acquired portfolios.

Please make the following <u>available</u> upon our arrival at the bank:

1. Merchant processing policy and procedure manuals.

2. Committee minutes for merchant-related activities.

3. Recent reports issued by the bankcard associations.

4. Merchant files.

5.   Inventory logs for credit card equipment maintained for resale or lease to merchants.

6.   Agent bank files.

7.   All third-party credit files including current financial statements of ISOs/MSPs.

8.   All third-party written contracts and agreements, including contracts between ISOs/MSPs and the bank's data processor (if the bank does not have its own in-house operation).

9.   All Visa and MasterCard correspondence, including quarterly processing statements, pledge agreements, fraud monitoring reports, and chargeback monitoring reports.

10. Disaster contingency plans for third-party organizations and management's review of the plans.

11. Audit work papers

Appendix C: Profit and Loss Statement
(Sample Only)

VOLUMES (000's)	EXPENSES
Total Sales Volume	External Data Processing
Total Transactions	Internal Data Processing
Average Ticket	Research and Development
	Terminal Expense/Depreciation
INCOME	Personnel
Gross Merchant Discount	Telephone Expense
Interchange (-)	Occupancy Expense
Assessments (-)	Travel and Entertainment
Net Merchant Discount	Supplies
Interest Income	Professional Fees
Transaction Fees	Fraud and Chargeback Losses
Terminal Fees	Miscellaneous Expenses
Miscellaneous Fees	
Total Income	**Total Direct Expenses**
Total Income Per Transaction	Total Allocated Expenses
Return on Total Income	
Return on Total Expense	Total Expenses
Direct Expenses Per Transaction	**Net Contribution Before Tax**
Total Expenses Per Transaction (Unit Cost)	

Appendix D: Merchant File Review Worksheet

Merchant File Review Worksheet				
Merchant Name				
Merchant Application				
- Signatures				
- Business Type				
- Description of Product and Services				
- Average Ticket Size				
- Volume Information				
- Social Sec/Tax ID				
- Trade and Bank Refs				
- Current Processor				
- Time in Business				
- Proper Approval				
Site Verification				
- w/photo				
- Inspected by				
Credit Bureau Report				
Evidence of Previous Merchant Activity				
Check MATCH				
Purchase/Lease Equip				
Discount Rate				
% Swiped Transactions				

Glossary

Acquiring Bank - A bank that contracts with merchants to settle electronic transactions.

Agent Bank - A member of a bankcard association that agrees to participate in an acquirer's merchant processing program. The agent may or may not be liable for losses incurred on its merchant accounts. An agent is usually a small community bank that wants to offer merchant processing as a customer service. Agent banks that participate in an acquiring bank's program only insofar as to refer merchants are known as referral banks. Referral banks typically do not assume liability for merchant losses.

Authorization - An issuing bank's approval of a credit card transaction in a specific amount. If a merchant complies with bankcard association rules in obtaining an authorization, by telephone or electronic terminal, payment to the merchant is guaranteed.

Backroom Operations - Operational functions performed by the acquirer or issuer to facilitate the day-to-day processing of credit card transactions (e.g., settlement, fraud, and chargebacks).

Bankcard Association - Visa U.S.A., Inc. and MasterCard International Incorporated are bankcard associations. Banks must be members of an association to offer their credit card services. Membership rights and obligations are specifically defined by the associations. Both Visa and MasterCard require all members of their organization to be banks.

Bank Identification Number / Interbank Card Association (BIN/ICA) - A series of numbers used to identify the settling bank for both acquiring and issuing transactions.

Chargeback - Generated when a cardholder disputes a transaction or when the merchant does not follow proper procedures. The issuer and acquirer research the facts to determine which party is responsible for the transaction. Strict bankcard association rules must be followed.

Debit Card - A card that customers use to pay for a merchant's goods and services. A debit card also enables a user to transact business at an automated teller machine (ATM). In a debit card transaction, the cardholder is accessing funds from a personal checking or savings account. Debit card transactions can be on-line or off-line.

Discount Rate - The fee, as a percent of sales volume, an acquirer charges a merchant for processing sales transactions.

Electronic Benefits Transfer (EBT) - The electronic delivery of government benefits using plastic cards.

Electronic Data Capture - Process used when the merchant "swipes" the credit card through an electronic card reader or terminal. The information on the card's magnetic stripe is entered into the processor's database electronically.

Factoring - A form of fraud in which a merchant creates false sales transactions, inflates the sales amount, or alters the sales drafts to receive funds from the issuer. The merchant's intentions could be to obtain additional money to cover chargebacks or cash flow problems, or the merchant may have ceased operations and plans to abscond with the sales proceeds. If the merchant disappears, the acquirer would be responsible for any remaining chargebacks.

Future/Delayed Delivery - Sales transactions on products or services that are delivered in the future. Such products or services include airline tickets, concert tickets, and travel/tour packages.

Holdback - A percentage of the merchant's sales deposits that the acquirer holds back to serve as a reserve against future exposure or to cover existing chargebacks.

Independent Sales Organization (ISO) - An organization that provides a variety of merchant processing functions on behalf of the acquirer. These functions may include soliciting new merchant accounts, arranging for terminal purchases or leases, and providing backroom services. An ISO may also be referred to as a member service provider (MSP). The acquirer must register all ISOs/MSPs with the bankcard associations.

Interchange - The electronic infrastructure that processes financial and non-financial transactions between financial institutions.

Interchange Fee - A fee paid by one bank to another to cover handling costs and credit risk in a bank card transaction. The interchange fee, a percentage of the transaction amount, is derived from a formula that takes into account authorization costs, fraud and credit losses, and the average bank cost of funds.

Laundering - A form of fraud in which a merchant that holds an account with an acquirer submits drafts for a merchant that does not. The authorized merchant typically receives a percentage of the unauthorized merchant's sales volume. Several states' criminal statutes prohibit laundering.

Member Alert to Control High Risk Merchants (MATCH) - This file, formerly known as the combined terminated merchant file (CTMF), is maintained by the associations based on information reported by acquirers. By checking this file before approving a merchant, an acquirer determines whether the merchant has a history of poor operating practices.

Member Service Provider (MSP) - A nonmember of MasterCard who markets bankcard merchant acceptance on behalf of MasterCard financial institutions.

Merchant Processing - The settlement of electronic payment transactions for merchants. It is a separate and distinct business line from credit card issuing. Merchant processing activity, which is off-balance-sheet, involves gathering sales information from the merchant, collecting funds from the issuing bank, and paying the merchant. Various kinds of third parties may be involved.

Paper-based Transaction - An operation in which the merchant imprints the credit card and submits paper sales drafts to the acquirer for collection. The paper drafts are sent to the processing center where they are processed and transferred to magnetic tape for transmission through interchange.

Rent-a-BIN - An arrangement in which a bank permits ISO/MSPs to use the bank's BIN/ICA number for credit card issuing or merchant processing.

Retrieval Request - A form used to request a copy of the original sales draft from the merchant. A merchant that fails to send a copy of the sales draft may receive a chargeback. Such chargebacks are not appealable. Issuers might request a copy of the sales draft to verify the signature, to investigate the lack of an imprint, to carry out a cardholder's inquiry, or to look into the possibility of fraud.

Secured Socket Layers (SSL) - A protocol providing data security during transmission. SSL uses data encryption, server authentication, and message integrity.

Settlement - The process of transmitting sales information to the card-issuing bank, which collects funds and reimburses the merchant. Various third parties may be involved in all aspects of settlement.

Third-party Organization - Any outside company with which the acquirer contracts to provide merchant processing services. The services could include network and data transmissions, merchant accounting, backroom operations, sales, or customer service.

References

Regulations

12 CFR 3.10(d), Establishment of Minimum Capital Ratios for an Individual Bank

12 CFR 7.1017, National Bank as Guarantor or Surety on Indemnity Bond

12 CFR 21.11, Suspicious Activity Report

OCC Issuances

Advisory Letter 99-6, "Guidance to National Banks on Web Site Privacy Statements"

Advisory Letter 2000-9, "Third-Party Risk"

Advisory Letter 2000-12, "Risk Management of Outsourcing Technology Services"

Advisory Letter 2001-3, "Internet-Initiated ACH Debits/ACH Risks"

Banking Circular 187, "Financial Information on Data Processing Servicers"

Banking Circular 229, "Information Security"

Banking Circular 235, "International Payment Systems Risk"

Banking Circular 260, "Interagency Statement on EDP Service Contracts"

OCC 98-3, "Technology Risk Management"

OCC 98-31, "Guidance on Electronic Financial Services and Consumer Compliance"

OCC 98-38, "Technology Risk Management: PC Banking"

OCC 99-20, "Certification Authority Systems"

OCC 2001-47, "Third Party Relationships"